Anish Kapoor

Germano Celant

Anish Kapoor

Fondazione Prada
Edizioni Charta

This monograph was created to celebrate the Anish Kapoor exhibition held in November 1995 at the Fondazione Prada in Milan.

Artistic Consultant
Pandora Tabatabai Asbaghi

Scientific Research
Anna Costantini

Research Assistant
Paolo Cecchetto

Graphic Design
Pierluigi Cerri
with
Ginette Caron
Stéphanie Girard

Graphic Supervisor
Gabriele Nason

Editing Supervisor
Emanuela Belloni

Editing
Anna Albano

Translation of the Text by Germano Celant
Stephen Sartarelli

Press Office
Silvia Palombi Arte & Mostre, Milan
Cristina Pariset, Milan

Production
Amilcare Pizzi Arti grafiche,
Cinisello Balsamo, Milan

Photographic Credits
Anzai
Graziano Arici, Venice
Dan Barsotti
Hans Biezen
Jose Manuel Costa Alves
Federica De Angeli, Genoa
Dirk De Neef, Ghent
Tom Haartsen, The Netherlands
Robert Hausser, Mannheim
Eeva Inkeri
Larry Lame, New York
John Edward Linden, London
Attilio Maranzano, Rome
Susan Ormerod, London
Andrew Penketh, London
Georg Rehsteiner, Vufflens-le-Chateau
John Riddy, London
Philipp Rittermann, San Diego
Meidad Suchowolski, Tel Aviv
O. Vaering, Oslo
Stephen White, London
Gareth Winters, London
Hirosuke Yagi, Nagoya

Edizioni Charta
9, via Castelvetro – 20154 Milan
tel. 39-2-33.60.13.43/6
fax 39-2-33.60.15.24

Printed in Italy

I would like to thank Jeff Dyson and Tim Shutter who have worked with me for many years and who have taken my sometimes difficult notions seriously. Nicholas Logsdail, Barbara Gladstone, Bonnie Rubenstein, Sharon Essor, Elisabeth McCrae and Susan Waxman are all due my deepest thanks. Most importantly my thanks to my dearest wife Susanne Spicale and our daughter Alba without whom even less would be possible.

Anish Kapoor

Documenting in a monograph the creative evolution of an artist as complex as Anish Kapoor was an undertaking that required the help of many people, simply because of the wealth of material and scientific verification involved. First and foremost, I would like to thank Anish Kapoor whose willingness to communicate went far beyond the bounds of confidence and friendship. It would have been almost impossible for me to document his creative evolution without his constant help which made the experience most stimulating and enjoyable.

The monograph came into being thanks to the enthusiasm and energy of the Fondazione Prada in Milan, in the persons of Miuccia Prada and Patrizio Bertelli.

We would like to thank Pandora Tabatabai Asbaghi for her expertise in selecting and arranging the iconographical material, and to express our wholehearted gratitude to Pierluigi Cerri who, with Ginette Caron, created some inspired graphics.

Anna Costantini's drive and specialist knowledge contributed greatly to the scientific accuracy of the monograph. Finally, I was fortunate to have the support of Nicholas Logsdail and the Lisson Gallery, in London, as well as the collaboration of Bonnie Rubenstein. Together with Paolo Cecchetto, they gathered information and documents that made it possible to reconstruct Anish Kapoor's artistic career.

I would like to close by saying a warm thank you to Susanne and Alba, who make up Anish's other creative, fantasy world. Thank you all very much.

Germano Celant

Contents

Artist as Sacerdos

Germano Celant

The artist has a central place in the history of culture because he has the power to give new forms to matter, endowing it with new character. His ability to produce a continuous metamorphosis of the universe, on a microcosmic but greatly symbolic scale, makes him an architect, a director, of the generative processes. His prestige stems from the creativity with which he brings to life the threads of language, that complex system in which knowing and feeling evolve. Moving between sign and symbol, the artist connects himself integrally to myth. In touch with the exemplars and archetypes of history and life, and always inventing new representations of them, he is an initiate.

The transformation of life into new images, the granting of force and energy to forms and material, takes place through a ritual, the ritual of art, which qualitatively converts the formless whole into a sacred whole. The meaning of the artist's pursuit, then, lies in his revitalization of life's origins through an activity in harmony with the cosmic and universal order of time. For Anish Kapoor, the magic of artmaking lies in continually rethinking and re-presenting the exemplary act of creating a universe. That action departs from a symbolic centre whose foundations rest in myth, and in the knowledge of the secret of life.

What is myth? The definitions are many, but essentially myth relates to the force that created the world, and that keeps the world alive through a continuous process of renewal. In Western culture, this force corresponds to the Word, or the timeless mystical sound that created the universe. Myth is sacred and myth is word— "the word that, when repeated, corresponds to ultimate power."[1]

The knowledge and interpretation of myth and word (*mythos* actually means "word" in Greek) is entrusted to the priest, the *sacerdos* (the "giver of the sacred"), who, through ritual, seeks to give unitary form to the parts of a lost meaning, and thus to bring the human closer to the divine. In his search for the lost image, the image to be rediscovered, the artist resembles the *sacerdos*. He tries to reunite what is scattered and dispersed, dried up and spent, in order once again to locate the sources of the mystical force that supports existence. His concern is the power of that force, which he wants to regenerate and re-present. The enclosures that he creates are spaces in which it can be isolated. A consecrator of materials and forms, of spaces and architectures, he sets out to reconstruct the secret of life, the heritage of the word and of the divine.

Kapoor's constructive process first consists of sanctifying a space in which the fragments of the word—*verbum* or *mythos*—can be reunited, so as to verify this power and force through the simultaneity of the work's different elements. In *1000 Names*, 1979–80 (pp. 8–13), he seeks—as he has since his earliest mature work—to define an enclosed space, a territory, in which to isolate and reveal the energy of the sacred in all its countless denominations: *one thousand names*. The piece is a group of three-dimensional forms constituted of raw pigments of the primary colours, first red and white, later yellow and blue. Projecting out from floor and wall, these volumes evoke images—cone and mountain, half-sphere and dome, pyramid and volcano— that seem in transit between the abstract and the natural, the negative and the positive. The placement of the same configuration on the construction's different "horizons"—the floor and the wall—reveals the energetic charge, like the tip of an iceberg, in the word—or *name*—that participates in the sacred or the myth.

In *1000 Names*, Kapoor, as artist/*sacerdos*, builds towers and pyramids to unite the heavenly and earthly, the human and the divine. He attempts, then, to decipher the mystery of *elsewhere*—to reveal the magnetism of the dialogue between the complementary forces and powers of above and below, here and there, the known and the unknown. These forces yield a form-generating current that manifests the movement of life. That current's infinitude overflows the limits of any language, real or abstract. In this sense the chromatic volumes of *1000 Names* can be seen as self-sufficient and self-generating, beyond any subjection to anthropomorphism, for they are full of an extrapersonal expressiveness that stems from the mutability of both the human and the divine.

Asserts Kapoor: "with the early powder pieces, one of the things I was trying to do was to arrive at something which was as if unmade, as if self-manifest, as if there by its own volition."[2] He also says, "I've always felt that my work had to be about something else and that's what saved it. I began to evolve a reasoning, which had to do with things being partially revealed. While making the pigment pieces, it occurred to me that they form themselves out of each other. So I decided to give them a generic title, *1000 Names*, implying infinity, a thousand being a symbolic number. The pigment works sat on the floor or projected from the wall. The pigment on the floor defines the surface of the floor and the objects appear to be partially submerged, like icebergs. That seems to fit the idea of something being partially there."[3] The conception of *1000 Names* subsists in a complex symbolic universe that revolves around the idea of the transit or passage (*in-betweenness*) from one dimension to another. The bounded room or space in which the work is situated can be seen as an inner "world," and this establishes an equivalence between the microcosmic and the macrocosmic, the human and the universal. The space, then, is existential and metaphysical, individual and

1000 Names, 1979-80

1000 Names, 1980

mystical. Its walls symbolize the world's vectors, east, west, north, and south, which, at their points of intersection, the corners, allow the meeting of the human and the superhuman. Within them, on the floor and on the wall, Kapoor's multiple forms of different-coloured chromatic powder together constitute a nongeometric whole, open and free.

The grouping and the placement of these figures in such a space reflect a primordial totality, the existence of which is unconditioned and in flux. Like a small holy mountain, each entity rises from the ground to establish a harmony between earth and heaven. Each element is constructed, directly or indirectly, from a powder of pure colour, which rests on a form or supports it, creating an aureole around it.

This pigment signifies the creative force; it is a sign of life, like seed or pollen. Suggesting the birth and growth of a fruit that may assume any form or character, it suggests the mutability of life, the pressure on all subjects, spiritual and physical, to become embodied as something else. The symbology of colour is infinite, ranging from the cosmic to the spiritual, from the biological to the ethical, from the religious to the mystical. In every culture, colour restates the constant of luminous energy, of light, a recurrent motif in all articulations of metaphysics—the prime visible manifestation of the life force and of the divine. "With the early powder works I was much more concerned with the way the objects gave out light; they seem to be a source of light."[4]

In *1000 Names*, opposites and complementaries, light and dark, are reconciled not only through colour-light but through the passage between upper and lower, outer and inner, surface and subterranean—all integral parts of a work on the ground or on the wall. The horizon line on which the elements rest or from which they project is by definition a point of transition between two worlds. It is also a surface of motion: by walking on the floor, one ritually redefines the adventure of life, one's movement through the world, one's journeys, one's existential pilgrimages. In standing on the ground, the forms and volumes of pigment, besides calling attention to the poles of the known and the unknown, speak of art as growth, as a seed that develops and changes, ever susceptible to permutation. Art is seen as a living organism that mutates from embryo to maturity even while always remaining unique, whole, and integral. *1000 Names* becomes a place of the past, the present, and the future, a place where one may glimpse both roots sinking into the ground and the ebb and flow of a wandering aerial energy in the heavens. It is a work in a state of growth, with a vitality and an intimate essence of its own. Kapoor conceives it as a metaphor for an imaginary realm that is a space of perpetual transformation.

1000 Names, 1979-80

Moreover, this constellation of fragile, tactile elements in the womb of the floor implies an antimonumental logic more in keeping with the feminine principle than with the male. Gigantism and verticalism are absent, as are pure, absolute images. Instead, Kapoor chooses an open code that avoids the univocality almost always associated with obligatory symmetry, and also with the equally obligatory sorts of asymmetry. In addition, through its free, intuitive arrangement of forms and volumes the work makes a perceptible, urgent connection with the surrounding space. This connection indicates an identification with architecture, which serves as a centre of gravity, a *cavea* or womb for the convergence of introversion and extroversion, of feminine and masculine.

The whole of *1000 Names* can thus be taken as a figure of reconciliation between diverse sexualities, the locus of an androgynous body springing from a gathering of primordial fragments: "*1000 Names* implies that the objects are part of a much bigger whole. The objects seem to be coming out of the ground or out of the wall, the powder defining a surface, implying that there is something below the surface, like an iceberg poking out of the subconscious."[5] Full of conscious and unconscious vitality, this presence lays claims to be infinite. For it posits the creative process not as an operation of abstraction or reduction (as in the Minimalist approach, which set up a rigid, functional relationship with the exhibition space and architecture) but rather as a way of respecting the existence that flows in the space, of establishing an organic, perceptible relationship with the real, without preconceptions and irrespective of genre.

What is the source of this energetic, enigmatic vision of art as sacrifice and rite, in which the artist presents himself as a *sacerdos* and the work as a tool of the evolution and transformation that will enable the individual and society to realize their unrealized potential? What sort of artistic or philosophical experience is Kapoor referring to in *1000 Names*, a hermetic, magical environment born of the *conjunctio oppositorum* of conscious and unconscious, day and night, male and female, active and passive, life and death? From what existential and creative precedents arose this need to build a bridge between opposite and complementary poles, establishing a flow of energy between art and life?

Kapoor was born in Bombay in 1954, of an Indian father and a Jewish mother. After attending primary schools, he enrolled in an engineering school for six months, then, when he was about eighteen, left to devote himself to painting: "I had been painting when I was in India."[6] In 1973 he went to study in England, enrolling at Hornsey College of Art, where he remained until 1977. In 1978 he went on to postgraduate study in the sculpture department of the Chelsea School of Art.

During this period Kapoor read Carl Jung with great interest. He also met Paul Neàgu, a Rumanian artist working in Edinburgh and London who had come into contact with Joseph Beuys on the occasion of the German artist's *Celtic (Kinloch Rannoch) Scottish Symphony* project, at the Edinburgh College of Art in August 1970, and had continued to follow him up to the time of his show "The Secret Block," which toured England and Scotland in 1974. Kapoor fully acknowledges Neàgu's influence on his perception of art as a ritual, ecstatic process: "There was someone I found very important to me then, Paul Neàgu. He really had a lot to do with the way my growth as a person occurred. He was a foreigner working in this context here, that had something to do with it. He opened my eyes to the idea that making art wasn't about making more or less beautiful things and that there was some deeper purpose to it."[7]

An initial inventory of Kapoor's lexical materials can be seen in *Untitled*, 1975 (p. 5), a work executed at Hornsey. It consists of a human half-figure, half-male, half-female, drawn on the floor in white chalk and run through by a long iron rod, from which radiate a metal foot covered in chalk and a number of "rays," also in chalk and iron, which interweave with the words "male" and "female" and support simple volumetric figures such as spheres and cubes, or parts of them—angles and half-spheres, concave and convex forms. The work's visual orchestration, then, is based on a harmony of elements that coexist in the same space and have a common matrix (the body), from which they emanate like an aura of forms and materials. The force rising from the ground is absolutely physical, and its physicality is magnetic: acting like the head of a comet, it both pulls along and emits a whole constellation of sculptures.

To designate this process of the dismemberment of the individual (and social) organism in plastic visual motifs, Kapoor combines the Duchampian figuration of *Étant Donnés: 1. la chute d'eau 2. le gaz d'éclairage*, 1948–49, with the iconography and process orientation of Beuys, who in *Manresa*, 1966, exhibited a half-cross on the wall, and who made much use of iron rods and chalk in such works as *Eurasia 32. Satz der Sibirischen Symphonie*, 1969. Kapoor, however, is not interested simply in referring to iconography or process; rather, his attentions are focused on both artists' philosophical and alchemic obsessions. "One artist who was very important to me was Duchamp. Not the Duchamp of the readymade but the Duchamp of *The Large Glass (The Bride Stripped Bare by Her Bachelors, Even)* and *Etant Donnés*, the Duchamp of Alchemy… a perfect kind of oppositeness. I made quite a lot of work that had to do with this polarity."[8]

1000 Names, 1979-80

Attempting to probe Kapoor's metaphor of a body on the ground, which also acts as the source of elements that break away from it to rise toward the heavens, one may identify a dialectic between a stable element—the prison of this androgyne's individuality, however absolute that individuality is—and a volatile one: the divine, the sacred, which is both separated from and connected to the body by the bar of rays. Kapoor tends to emphasize connection. He wants to abolish difference—he wants material's errant force to contain both the sacred and the human. Rift is transformed into fusion, the body becoming a shining star around which instantaneous radiations of molecules gather to become form and volume— "the body being the central theme, the body being the vessel, in which the transformation takes place."[9] In the *Untitled* of 1975, however, the problem is still one of separation, so much so that the body is as much a centrifugal force as a centripetal one. While it supports the work's materials and forms, it is equally penetrated by them in its symbolic orifices; it is not yet a glorious body fused into a total unity, cut from a sacred, ritual self-sufficiency, as in *1000 Names* (pp. 24–25).

The incompleteness of the transition is expressed in the figure's androgyny, and in the fact that it is only half drawn in, not fully realized. But this figure is on the road to completion, and is combined with a recognizable, literally weighty bodily presence: the metal foot, metaphor for a slow, ponderous advance toward the final outcome. *Untitled* of 1975 is a pivotal work in Kapoor's gradual definition of art as a casting off of one's own identity in favour of a golden, numinous state, in which the body is transformed into a lymph of the Tree of Life, and of Art.

In the articulation of this *Untitled*, the drawing of the androgyne becomes an archetypal image of the human psyche. The androgyne appears as the primordial unity predating the separation of the genders, the "double" whole in which all opposites converge. Its presence as a white shadow on the floor represents the life-breath—the "rays" as breaths—that will eventually give rise to Kapoor's later vocabulary of forms and materials: cube, sphere, chalk, powdered pigment. His work will thrive on the dialogue between spirit and matter, above and below, masculine and feminine, for it is in *duality* that the energy of transformation and evolution lies. Only from the double can the centrifugal power of being arise, the infinite dance of an art that proclaims itself as self-generating, impulsive, mobile, and open to secret and enigma. In *Untitled* Kapoor illuminates a holistic vision based on an osmosis between self-impregnating opposites, an interrelationship of inside and outside, superficial and subterranean, conscious and unconscious. This vision will continue to take shape in *To Reflect an Intimate Part of the Red*,

1000 Names, 1979-80

Untitled, 1977

Untitled, 1976

1981 (pp. 50–53), *Mother as a Mountain*, 1985 (p. 78), *Here and There*, 1987 (pp. 165–67), *The Healing of St. Thomas*, 1989 (p. 117), *Void Field*, 1989, and *When I Am Pregnant*, 1992 (pp. 165–67).

At the centre of all Kapoor's art lies the pregnancy of the absent body—shadow, aura, and void. Renouncing the fullness and completeness of sculpture and painting, he seeks a mirror-state in which the artist becomes a nomad, the protagonist of "mnemic migrations"[10] among the formal and material languages with which he asserts a presence in the world. ("I am a painter who is a sculptor," says Kapoor.[11]) The notion of cutting the body into fragments of matter, of reducing it to a simple expression of the symbolic, underscores the constant presence of an *interval* marking the passage between material and immaterial, between mobility and immobility. The figures in the world of the body's transmutation are memories of the idea of the flame-body, in which the human being is accepted as a residual figure.

In *Table of Dreams*, 1976, the idea of the body's absence, indirectly harking back to the "unspoken voices" of Brancusi's table, is accompanied by the energetic physical presence of a sculpture halfway between soft and hard, between flesh and object. In this drama of laceration and flux, however, there is a yearning for a primordial cohesion. This confusion is overcome in *Untitled*, 1977 (pp. 2–3), a sort of vulval enclosure or screen made of painted cloth held up by poles, and functioning as both a construction and a site of ceremony; and also in another untitled work of the same year, a chair occupied by a vaginal metal container, and surrounded by and connected to white-painted poles surmounted by spheres of cloth made solid with plaster. Both works delimit a space (in order to bring it back to life), as much with their ceremonial poles as with the soft bed of Mother Earth—the natural-fibre cotton cloth. This enclosed inner space of salvation invokes the isolation required of the initiate. At the same time, it is also a wedding chamber, an open room, decorated with branches and flowers, in which the couple settles down on a rude bed to create a third being. A Duchampian itinerary returns in another *Untitled* of 1977, in which a dark-coloured tent separates two worlds while also suggesting a visual bridge between them. On one side an object of steel and chalk rises from the ground; from it radiates a line of linkage, exceeding the limits of the tent. On the other side is a platform, also standing on the ground, on which rest a mirror and some soft instruments. The joining of these two universes of hard and soft, masculine and feminine, is enhanced by the deafening noise of a kind of mechanical metronome that beats a stick against the ground, turning sound into an alchemic coagulant.

Anthropomorphic Ritual, 1977

Untitled, 1977

Aside from their repeated echo of Duchamp's *Large Glass*, and of the Jungian idea of the ritual encounter and "internal marriage" of male and female as a fundamental process of the human condition,[12] the configurations of these works express Kapoor's desire to arrive at a formal middle-ground between the meanings of the body and of its absence, between stasis and potential activity. This ground is to be achieved through abstract forms and soft volumes that are no longer representations of transformation, evolution, life, and growth, but rather are simply paradigms of the construction and unveiling of the inner state of a being in the world. In this series of untitled works, Kapoor is concerned with a casting off of the body, a progress from the fullness of physical and tactile energy typical of *arte povera* to the emptiness of metaphysical vertigo. Plunging into his materials as so many pneumas nourishing life, he begins to pose the question of art as infinite growth, as in *1000 Names*. His evolution along this path finds another confirmation in recent art: the "environments" of Paul Thek, whose *Procession in Honor of Aesthetic Progress: Object to Theoretically Wear, Carry, Pull, or Wave*, 1968, and *Stag in the Boat*, 1971–72, provided considerable iconographic and poetic inspiration for Kapoor's early works. "I was very interested at the time in Paul Thek. His is a sad story but he was a marvelous artist. I never saw one [of his environments] for real then, only in art magazines, but I think what was important about them to me was that they were deeply ritualized situations."[13]

In *Anthropomorphic Ritual*, 1977, a group of airy configurations float in the void, rising like birds, or fantastical creatures with strange wings and beaks, from a womb of painted cloth. Images of flight subtending a birth, and separated from the earthly, vulval bed, they are in direct spiritual contact with the heavens. In the guise of fragments and disparate forms, there emerges from the organ's slit a full image (or word) that spills over to the outside as visual energy. Out of the open body comes a coloured swarm of light, ascending objects heading out into space. They rise up in search of a landscape in which to settle.

Another untitled work of 1977, on the other hand, is a physical realization o the idea of a descent into a context: here the forms aspire to land on earth, once they have found a territory to house them. Suspended from a wire, figures of coloured fabric loom, as if about to land, over a painted surface, again vulval in form, that is also occupied and cluttered with other objects. Here and in *Anthropomorphic Ritual*, Kapoor once again establishes a balance or duality between opposite yet mutually attractive elements. Maintaining the dialectic between divine and human, spiritual and physical, angelic and satanic, he makes forms fly and at the same time descend. He maintains a cyclical vision that rests on the meeting of earth and ether, low and high, dust and air. The archetype of the glorious body is transformed through the dialectical relationship between the volatile and the stable. This transformation coincides with a release of free imagistic energy, but, at the same time, also corresponds to a reabsorption and freezing of the surround. If the power of the images is to circulate freely and unobstructed, the territorial web must become compact, enclosed, so as to attract these liberated objects, figures, fragments, and forms. An opening requires a closing, a fullness wants a void, the limitless demands a limit.

In 1978, before completing his studies at the Chelsea School of Art, Kapoor created an untitled installation in his studio that marked a moment of transition from his early work to the more mature *1000 Names*. The piece was made up of fragments of chalk, electric motors, silks, and Jackson Pollock-like strokes on two large transparent screens that divided the room, filtering a view of several stands on which stood small spheres. Every plane of the room from floor to walls was penetrated by a constellation of two- and three-dimensional signs, an aggregation that took full and uninterrupted possession of the space. It was as though secretions and humours originating in the body had found a mode of total, almost cosmic respiration, magical and enigmatic, forming a full, self-contained universe.

Between 1975 and 1978, a wellspring of energy and art had led to the transmutation of the figure of the androgyne into a sensual organ capable of granting coloured forms and figures their freedom and access to the air. In *Untitled*, 1978–79, this energy generates a proliferation of images so rich as to fill up an entire *alveus* or space. Here all opposites coexist: dispersion and accumulation, surface and volume, solidity and transparency, colour and material, mobile and immobile, geometric and organic, low and high, gesture and plan, order and anarchy, fullness and emptiness. One melts into the other, merging in a disconnected agglomerate that strives to reconstitute itself as a higher unity. Objects on the ground, like signs on the wall and floor, present themselves as metaphors of a multidirectional force. A terrific ebullition begins to register the fits and starts of a body in a state of fusion, transmuted into base matter but tending to become *One*. As in the alchemic tradition of *solve et coagula*, art is the vehicle of a renewed energy the purpose of which is to transform the elementary body, which underlies works from the *Untitled* of 1975 to that of 1978–79, into a supreme, sublime body, as in *1000 Names*. The metamorphic journey is complete, and the material distilled can now shine within itself in celebration of both the sacred and the profane, the divine and the human.

Untitled Installation, 1978

1000 Names, 1979-80

The Garden of Origins

The pure image, unscathed by the act of coming into being, is an extreme experience. Kapoor identified it in 1979, on a return visit to India, where he discovered primary colour in its raw state. In its perfect alloy, this material corresponded to his search for an absolute metaphysical language—a language capable of melding together in unity the parts of the glorious body, which is composed of superior fragments that together solidify the multiple complexity of the universe.

Using this powdered pigment, Kapoor succeeds, in *1000 Names*, in transforming symbol into reality, in rendering metaphors of light and creation as physicalized events, integrating their polarities. "What I did discover in India was a material," he says.[14] Aside from material, however, Indian culture also provided him with a confirmation of his poetic and philosophical orientation: "I hadn't realized that the direction I had been working in was already there. I was only there for a month or so, but it was a real affirmation of my being… The whole of the Indian outlook on life is about opposite forces. One thing I was fascinated by were the little shrines and temples by the roadside, which are all over India, and are specifically orientated towards this dualistic vision."[15] In India, moreover, the transformation of every gesture or act into a sacred serial rite helped Kapoor to reclaim for himself an infinite, virtual procedure—*1000 Names* inaugurated a ceremony of chromatic and formal reinvention and expansion that would last until 1985—and to understand the destiny of his art: "I do not want to make sculpture about form—it doesn't really interest me. I wish to make sculpture about belief, or about passion, about experience that is outside of material concern."[16]

In the culture of Kapoor's origins, the numinous permeates all reality; in the Hindu cosmogony, gods such as Shiva are omnipresent. And the wall decorations in Indian temples are inscribed within a philosophical vision of the fecundity and abundance of the regenerative spirit. Kapoor's return to these origins confirmed his desire to identify art with a transformative will that, floating between painting and sculpture, rises up in the world to permeate every order of object and landscape: "I think I am a painter who is a sculptor."[17]

The *substantia* of the painting-sculptures that would result is pure pigment, which, despite its optical weight as dense colour, has a soft, ethereal quality that makes the features and contours of volume and form nebulous. It dissolves considerations of the real and emphasizes the power of light, which becomes a shimmering, a vibration, that allows the forms to float in space like Monet's waterlilies, or to dissolve in a rarefied atmosphere, as in a

Turner landscape. The works are full but vaporous, like red, white, and yellow dandelions erupting from the floor, producing a visual vortex that swallows up the gaze. Being formed by the purest of powder, the contours of each element become labile, the surfaces vulnerable, changeable, indefinite. By transforming sculpture into a restless vibrant mass, an unstable, fragile object, Kapoor makes his own contribution toward moving beyond the disagreeable rigidity and absolutism of Minimal art. He situates himself in a kind of symbolic and procedural syntony with *arte povera*, and with Land art from Jannis Kounellis to Robert Smithson, enriching their vocabulary of sensorial and sensual data. First of all, his vibrant, seductive images, which invite one to draw close and touch, throw the visual closure of a Donald Judd or a Dan Flavin into crisis. The technologically produced surfaces of those artists' works offer crystalline or metallic skins. Kapoor instead presents an unstable, porous epidermis, fragmented and permeable, seeming both to float upon and to compose the sculpture's forms and volumes, which themselves seem to float in space.

Kapoor's desire is to enter the thing itself. For in the esoteric tradition, art is an image that approaches completeness but does not reach it. It must always be perceived as integrated with something beyond its self-presentation. In *1000 Names*, then, colour defines form but does not resolve it. It slowly makes one recognize its existence, but the aureole that surrounds it also demonstrates its contingency and ephemerality. The quest for the sacred is expressed in the pilgrimage or journey toward the wellsprings of sight. Colour offers one route toward understanding the shape of the power and energy that inform the universe. It cannot, however, tolerate any absolute definition, but must obey the laws of the movement and flow of life. Aspiring to connect with that process of compression and expansion, the pigments of *1000 Names* amass like unstable entities, breathing with the earth. Their pulverization, their mixing of earth and air, allows each object to situate itself at the juncture between the physical and the metaphysical, the measurable and the immeasurable, matter and spirit. Finally the brightness, the impetuous, elusive fibrillation of the individual red, yellow, and blue— the latter of an intensity recalling Yves Klein's cosmic sensibility—have a powerful sense of purity, showing that they belong to the realm of pure Idea: art as the epiphany of the Sublime.

Closed within the perimeter of its energy charge, subject to the law of the "symbolic," *1000 Names* embodies the advent of a "mindscape" and of a "soulscape."[18] It presents itself as the ceremony of an illumination of life and creativity. The colours foreground their own allegorical quality: in Kapoor's personal symbology, red becomes a symbol of masculinity and the

As if to Celebrate I Discovered a Mountain Blooming with Red Flowers, 1981

Mother as a Mountain, 1985

generative, white refers to virginity and the feminine, and yellow corresponds to desire (the passional, solar part of red). At the same time, Kapoor's self-renewing forms become vehicles of a *theatrum chemicum* in which one rediscovers the buried archetypes that will revitalize the continuity between culture and life.

The first version of *1000 Names*, exhibited in 1980 in the Paris studio of the sculptor Patrice Alexandre, consisted of objects made directly of red and white pigment. This was followed by a show at the Coracle Press in London, in which Kapoor broadened his vocabulary of forms and colours while preserving the impact of an arrangement that fills a space to the point of transforming it into an energy field. Other permutations and modifications followed, the essence and variety of the work being in a constant state of enrichment between 1981 and 1985.

At the same time that he continued to work on ephemeral installations, Kapoor also began to broaden the iconography of his petrified, primordial landscapes. In 1981 he created *As If to Celebrate I Discovered a Mountain Blooming with Red Flowers* (p. 55), *To Reflect an Intimate Part of the Red* (pp. 50–53), and *Part of Red* (pp. 45–49). For their forms, these works employ pure figures such as the sphere and the parallelepiped, and they assume a more articulated iconography than the earlier works did–from stair and mountain to dome and enclosure. It is here that Kapoor's colours are first enriched with the addition of blue. Also, in both the number of their elements and the spaces they delimit, the groupings in these works are simpler and more contained than the earlier ensembles; the visual areas they describe fall under one's gaze more easily. Unlike *1000 Names*, they no longer immerse one in an archipelago of forms and colours, instead confronting one with a sculptural presence.

In essence, the figures that start to emerge in 1981 recall the symology of the works of 1975–79. They too present hemispheric cavities and oval or roundish constructions that evoke the female body, as though Kapoor, after his intense self-discovery of 1979 steeped in a variety of cultural stratifications, wanted to reintroduce fragments of the unconscious and to point to profound, unexpressed meanings. These works present the dome as an absolute symbol of the whole as sacred enclosure and uterus, locus of the feminine and the Great Mother, inexhaustible reservoir of psychic and erotic energy, source and origin of all becoming, all evolution. Other spatial archetypes, from stairs to mountains, recall ascensional—male—dynamics, as well as the desire for flight, the aspiration to transcendence, and the constellations of the psyche. Even the perception of landscape changes: "I began to be very interested in the whole idea of landscape; what is

1000 Names, 1980

1000 Names, 1979-80

Study of the artist, 1985

formalistic landscape, what is the energized idea of external space, which is the equivalent to the energized idea of internal space, one of the most important areas is the garden. I began to look at very reduced gardens, of course sand gardens, but perhaps the most important influence was from Persian carpets."[19]

If in *1000 Names* the rhythm of change was relentless, unceasingly living, breathing, and passing through successions of different moments corresponding to new situations, here it contracts nearly to the point of petrifaction. The morphological transformations of the *natural* matrix that permeates *As If to Celebrate I Discovered a Mountain Blooming with Red Flowers* are such as to make this group of "mountains" seem crystallized, as much by their abstract, geometrical formalization as by their concentration at the centre of the space. The work refers to a haiku, and reflects a Zen vision of the world, but the sense of reawakening induced by its Duchampian, Eastern play of words is more important. In this sense *As If to Celebrate . . .* should be confronted as a further questioning of art.

For Kapoor, art cannot be immutable, cannot continue to produce the same *names*. It must *reawaken*. His effort in these works is to rouse his painting/ sculpture from the effect of gravity that threatened to submerge it in *1000 Names* and to rediscover an iconic spontaneity based on the light of *living* images. The 1982 works *Red in the Centre* (pp. 60–63) and *White Sand, Red Millet, Many Flowers* (p. 59), and the 1983 *Six Secret Places* (pp. 74–75), break out of any metaphysical schema of forms and materials and return to the capturing of a recognizable image, or at least a "figural" one. These configurations rising from the ground reflect a pulsing unconscious magma. The objects and forms seem to arise out of a subconscious imagery stratified in time, out of the artist's memory of his cultural, natural, and artistic roots. There are images of fire, of the body and of plants that manage to come together in symbolic unities of from five to seven elements. The works point to Kapoor's interest in memory, and in the freight of images that spring from history and culture.

In the sculptural experiments of 1981 and after, which run parallel to the variants of *1000 Names*, the need to master memory as a subjective reflection on one's own existence—as, in this case, an Indian-born artist active on the international scene—is of central importance. In particular, the theme of myth as testimony to a material, social, and spiritual life, a theme of Eastern origin, leads Kapoor slowly, until 1985, to choose and to live out an iconography that is ever more naturalistic: "Increasingly what is important is not looking at and reading myths as an observer, but *living* them, seeing connections with myths after the fact, so that one enters into those

Red in the Centre, 1982

The Chant of Blue, 1983

psychological states and ways of being that have made those myths."[20] The deciphering of these natural images continues to lie in combinations of opposites: high and low, damp and dry, mortal and immortal, raw and cooked, perishable and permanent. This coupling of antinomies both carries on Kapoor's chosen discussion of dualities and enriches it with a naturalistic symbolism that is global and universal in nature: "Binary oppositions are the fundamental elements of the human condition. Capturing the void in matter is one way of creating drama, of placing the scene in a physically and psychologically clear language, in the sense that every form is either concave or convex. The materials used in Indian art can be perishable, such as bread, rice, and clay, or durable, such as stone and precious metals."[21]

The struggle against time passes through the peace and quiet of the Oriental garden, a sanctuary of the memory of nature. The combination of sand and rock, moss and shrub, in these gardens symbolizes the perfect, balanced union of the elements of the universe. Kapoor looks at the gardens as he would at Oriental carpets, which reflect the "garden of heaven,"[22] and which consist of elements that coexist according to an "organic geometry and become an image of the earthly reflection of the heavenly state."[23] Intended as a place of ceremony, the Oriental garden is the site of powerful sensory impressions that put us in touch with cosmic energies. Kapoor therefore takes it as a "place of power,"[24] so much so that he considers his objects of powdered colour "functionaries of a garden."[25]

The image of the garden moves between the toils of agriculture and the pleasures of Eden, and is defined by a relationship of continuity and transfer between nature and culture. It is a "third nature,"[26] then—a figure that mirrors the androgyne. Kapoor recognizes the garden as a site for the kind of grafting and reconciliation of opposites that presides over his art. A place of both natural and artificial form, it is a laboratory in which they find an alchemic compatibility, can manifest a mutual sympathy, and thus achieve a circular, mythic mimesis. Myth returns in the reverberation of the images that take shape in *To Reflect an Intimate Part of the Red*, *White Sand, Red Millet, Many Flowers*, and *Red in the Centre*, and also in *Three*, 1982. These works evoke secret relations between vegetal forms and figures such as berries, seeds, leaves, fruits, and roots, as if the primary emulsion of the cubes and spheres in *1000 Names* were turning into a growth of organisms whose image mapped the artist's knowledge.

Colour remains central. The forms are arranged without hierarchy, but the group is organic, "almost fruitily organic,"[27] in character. The agglomerations become accumulations of naturistic travel notes, as if the garden functioned like an atlas, charting the gnosiological paths of the world. The forms Kapoor dreams up assume bizarre connotations, abandoning all reference to Minimalist reduction, for "they are going in the direction of the symbolic landscape."[28]

Like *To Reflect an Intimate Part of the Red*, *Part of the Red*, 1981, sets red at its centre. That colour is flanked by yellow, its erotic complement, and by blue, which, anchoring it to earth like a root, expresses the immaterial underground. The figures' iconography ranges from stairs and knots to fruit and seeds, suggesting the potentially infinite multiplication and range of this chromatic kernel, and bringing it to flower. Rising up impetuously, the forms also turn inward, exulting in their corollas, their living interior cavities. They propagate a *vivification* that transforms them into sensitive cells, the particles of a nervous system that branches out into the whole space: "Bodies keep coming into this internal landscape."[29]

In *White Sand, Red Millet, Many Flowers*, the efflorescence of the forms leads to an irradiation of points and protuberances that suggest shapes ranging from breasts to mountains. Creating a spell, an aura, not only of colour but of form, they give the object a seductive intimacy. In both this work and *To Reflect an Intimate Part of the Red*, the arrangements of elements refer strongly to their own depths. They call increasing attention to their curved, half-blossomed appearance, ardent and sensual, as if wishing to internalize, protect, and isolate themselves. In 1982 the vegetal objects and body parts become more resolved, growing and separating from the ground to become autonomous fruits, without any aureoles. The figure still refers inward, and no longer opens outward by dissolving into powder. Instead of breaking apart on the ground, it closes in on itself like some new being.

As the iconography broadens, the figures take on a solar quality, hot and dry. They even sometimes seem burned black—cold and raw, as close to death as to life. "The emphasis," according to Kapoor, "has shifted to the objects themselves so that they become like idols or 'objects of power.'"[30]

A protuberance jutting from the wall emphasizes the organic quality of language—the tongue, a characteristic of the Indian figurative tradition, particularly in reference to the goddess Kali, to whom Kapoor seems to be referring in the pyramid of breasts in *White Sand, Red Millet, Many Flowers*. Everywhere there is the same search for a life force, mystical and physical, universal and personal, which must be constantly illuminated so that it will not die out. This probing of different symbologies reevokes the power of female blackness (the woman who is reincarnated in the underworld, who is the world's life force), which appears in the pyramid in *White Sand, Red Millet, Many Flowers* and also in the subsequent *Black Earth*, 1983 (pp. 68–69). It is as if this woman were being given back a long-repressed, buried

The Pot is a God I, 1985

xxv

Hole and Vessel, 1983

voice: "As a man there's a feminine part to me, that's the creative and mysterious part."[31]

In every religion, the usual medium of communication between earth and heaven is the sacrificial rite. This contact, however, can assume different forms. In *1000 Names* made in 1982 (p. 57), and suggesting a sort of bud, seed, or heart, or some other internal organ, the material used is sky-blue-painted mud. This "heavy" work seems to deny the possibility of direct access to the divine—of any kind of contact with the divine that is more than symbolic. It signifies both renunciation and a joining of opposites—thus another "marriage." Kapoor's works from 1982 speak of fertility and the coming together of the sexes. The mediation no longer takes place vertically, from the earth to the heavens, but horizontally, like the attraction between women and men.

This earthly, carnal intercourse through mud, a material that unites the female principle (earth) and the male dynamic principle (water), has more than pleasure as its object: it also joins together diverse family groups, often held together by the magic number five, a sign of union and perfection. We see this in *Part of the Red*, *To Reflect an Intimate Part of the Red*, *Red in the Centre*, and *Full*, 1983. These ensembles seem to reflect a mystical vision of the earth as an *alveus* capable of spontaneously yielding its fruits and harvests of love and nourishment. In antiquity, between the woman as furrow and the man as cultivator, beautiful fruits were once produced. Demetre and Devi, the goddesses of agriculture and the woods, protected human union and preserved seed in the womb.

Kapoor's iconography in these works is strongly sexual. In *In Search of the Mountain*, 1985, and a version of *1000 Names* from the same year, for example, his symbols become phallic and vaginal—yet they simultaneously assume absolute geometrical forms, arriving at an excess of "geometric figuration" that makes them seem rigid and cold. Despite this involution, however, which seems to bar the possibility of creation, the works nevertheless give rise to another idea of creativity (or maternity): that of the womb as vessel and locus of natural growth (as in *Mother as a Mountain*), and of darkness and the void as the zero point of creation, where the name and the word are reborn. "Let's think of the first person who made a pot. I feel that it was almost certainly a woman. Let us say that she went to the riverside and found a lump of clay and was able, with a few subtle movements of her hands, to transform it into a pot. What has happened is that the clay is completely changed. It is now a pot. It has a new function, a new purpose and—what's most important—a new name. The ability to give a new name is, in a way, this act of transformation."[32]

The polished hardness of *Pot is a God* and *Pot for Her*, 1985 (p. 71), is the result of a refinement and crystallization of the dryness of epidermal sensuality in favour of a visceral sensuality. As the locus—the feminine locus—of mystery and enigma, the place where the wonders and secrets of all metamorphosis converge, place of the unmanifest and the unknown, the vessel is the *absolute* space. That void—wellspring and abyss, maelstrom and fullness of being—is presented as the maximum of unknown intensity. Furthermore, by depriving his objects of the chromatic vibrancy previously conferred on them by powdered colour, and creating openings and cuts in them, as in *Place*, 1985 (p. 79), Kapoor upsets the object's defensive perimeters, dissolving its texture and weight and making it transparent and luminous. This loss of solidity enables him to lay bare the object's interiority: "I have always engaged with interiority, that which is inside… Interiority has become evident, whereas with the early work it was implied."[33] With *Here and There* and *I* in 1987 and *Wound* in 1988 (p. 85), the concept and vision of interiority become a kind of zero point that precedes form and colour, but that implies every possible formal universe. Here Kapoor begins to think of emptiness and darkness as moving toward fullness. He moves from abstraction to concreteness, not the other way round. Emptiness becomes a concrete language through which creation reverses its process, does not come into the light but goes toward the shadows into which all worlds ultimately fall.

The Architecture of the Self

For Kapoor, the passage from emptiness to fullness must be physicalized in material. At the same time, if this material is to convey emptiness, it must be dematerialized. To maintain the presence of this dematerialized material, Kapoor needs a substance not airy or light but dense and heavy, hard and solid: stone. Interiority must clash with a hostile, crystallized tumescence, must descend deep inside it to take possession of its *spirit*, and to find there an *elsewhere* in which metaphysics is part of natural existence. This journey into the underside of things is a continuation of Kapoor's search to contain, within a vessel, a unity based on the duality between the ego and the nonego, the inside and the outside, spirit and matter. The artistic ceremony that Kapoor begins in 1987 continues the myth of oppositional dyads changing places by spilling over into each other, so that the negative becomes positive, full becomes empty, heavy becomes light.

The belief that the infinite is the other side of the finite is fully formulated in *I*, a large limestone boulder carved out inside to form a cavity. A hole above the cavity allows one a view into it—a view into a deep blue. The visual

Shrine, 1987

XXVII

experience is of looking at a nucleus of solid rock with a black circle on top, which, as one approaches, turns into an orifice, an opening onto a dark abyss. Similar to this, though with greater bodily emphasis, is the dialectic between inside and outside in *Wound*, 1985, where the stone is "wounded" and displays a pair of open red lips to the viewer's gaze. Both works carry on the artist's concern with the mechanism of life as a play of antagonistic poles, like Eros and Thanatos. In the one, nature displays the dual condition of presence and absence, wholeness and nothingness; in the other, nature shows that the inert—stone—can be reanimated, rediscovering a lost spiritual and fleshly potency.

The immersion in the dark chasm of infinite blue, like that in the red lips in which every principle of life, pure and impure, collects and coagulates, demonstrates the continuity in Kapoor's surrender to the metamorphic flux of material in the body and of the body in material. "I seem to be moving from light to darkness. I think I know why that is. One of the things that has always had a very strong pull for me has been what I might call a matriarchal view of creativity, of energy. It seems to me that that is towards darkness, perhaps toward the womb. . . Darkness is formless."[34]

Whether sculpture has a frontal individuality, as in *I*, or a fleshly presence, as in *Blood Stone*, 1988 (p. 91), stone, like mud, transforms it into a "real landscape"[35] rather than a "mindscape"—a labyrinth of forms and materials in which one loses oneself in order to find oneself (*1000 Names*)—or a magic or ritual circle releasing energy from its centre (*Part of the Red*). It becomes instead a cosmic solidification, a great being asserting itself by its imposing presence. The very verticality and weightiness of the stones, hollowed out and charged inside with blue or red, presuppose a permanence that symbolically underlies their relative immortality, as compared to the impermanence of the arrangements of raw pigment. On the other hand, the works' scale is now of a human dimension and status: "An essential issue in my work is that the scale always relates to the body. In the pigment works from 1979 to 1983, a sense of place was generated between the objects. This place has now moved inside the object so it has been necessary to change the scale. The place within is a mind/body space. A shrine for one person."[36]

Contemplation means not only venturing and losing oneself along the unknown, mysterious path formed by a constellation of enigmatic and natural, esoteric and corporeal figures, as in *1000 Names*; it also implies confronting a *solidified* spirit, a *solidified* infinity, which can no longer be rarefied. The use of stone confirms this need to recognize the *real* equivalence between mortality and immortality, and the need to crystallize the sacred instead of dissolving it. In the history of religion, the greatest

Void Field, 1989

Madonna, 1989-90

Installation, 1989; Angel, 1989;
Void Field, 1989

manifestations of the sacred have been lithic, from the Semitic bethels and the Arabian Kaaba to the black stone of Anatolia to Mithras, the Indo-Iranian lithic light. In the legend of Deucalion and Pyrrha, even the human is symbolized by stone. For all these reasons, one might say that stone is the path from the human to the divine. In *I*, the individual meets his destiny as something crude and heavy as well as sublime and redeemed; he comes up against his double, the I, who reclaims the body as a vehicle of the unknown. He is driven to awaken and to test himself against a thick wall erected between himself and the void, which swallows and devours all.

This nothingness or void can arouse a mixture of fear and awe. As a boundary, it is close to dream and hallucination, to ecstasy and trance—so much so that in *Earth*, 1991, and *Descent into Limbo*, 1992, it will present itself as an opening between light and darkness, an orifice in which human beings can lose themselves and fall. "Void is really a state within. It has a lot to do with fear, in Oedipal terms, but more so with darkness. There is nothing so black as the black within. No blackness is as black as that. I am aware of the phenomenological presence of the void works but I am also aware that phenomenological experience on its own is insufficient. I find myself coming back to the idea of narrative without storytelling, to that which allows one to bring in psychology, fear, death and love in as direct a way as possible. This void is not something which is of no utterance. It is a potential space, not a non-space."[37]

Seen in psychological terms, this is the dichotomy and the antithesis between the two planes of consciousness and unconsciousness. It reflects an awareness of the tangle of forces inside one, by which one is possessed. At the same time, the interval, the *in-betweenness*, that in earlier work held constellations of objects together is for the first time sucked inside. In a rising progression, the light that illuminated and penetrated the sculptures from 1983 to 1986, through a kind of mysterious metempsychosis, is transformed into darkness.

If one considers that behind these transformations stands the human individual—the *I*, who moves about in nature—then one can say that the initiation has reached its maturity. In both light and shadow, the subject has succeeded in recapturing the face of the divine. Having eliminated that separation, which is given in the passage through the very door of life itself—the maternal, sexual orifice—the human can now declare himself born: *Adam*, 1988–89. Following the recapture of *I* we see a crystallization of a higher illumination in which the human can be reintegrated, completing a kind of crossing that involves him down to his innermost fibers: *At the Hub of Things*, 1987, the first half-sphere in fibreglass, covered in dense Prussian

Untitled, 1993

Untitled, 1991; Mountain, 1991

xxx

blue pigment. This work begins the series of "Voids," which include *Madonna*, 1989–90 (pp. 114–15), whose monumental and architectural proportions (it is three metres in diameter) make it loom over anyone who approaches, the three elements of *Untitled*, 1990, and *Eyes Turned Inward*, 1993 (pp. 158–59). To allow for the epiphanic reabsorption of the human by the divine, these works turn the void outward. The enormous mass of blue, and the object's concave shape, create a kind of vertical abyss, capturing energy and pulling in the observer's gaze, if not his entire body.

The idea is "to make an object which is not an object, to make a hole in the space, to make something which actually does not exist."[38] Even more, the extraordinary appearance, loved and feared, of a piece of the void, at once finite and infinite, reactivates the symbolic contact between inside and outside, earth and heaven, male and female, active and passive, conceptual and physical, thus renewing the process of knowing. "The neophyte can, in this manner, have an effect on this unstable universe of powers that are outside him and inside him. The symbol, for him, is like a magical, irresistible entrance into that amorphous, tumultuous tangle of forces. [By means of] the symbol he enchains them, dominates and dissolves them; [by means of] the symbol he gives form to the infinite possibilities lying at the bottom of his unconscious, the unexpressed fears, the primordial impulses, the ancient passions."[39]

The plunge into the depths entails losing oneself, or experiencing a "sensual uncertainty."[40] One is also aware of being pulled into the magical vortex of an energy mass. "I have always felt drawn," says Kapoor, "towards some notion of fear in a very visual sense, towards sensations of falling, of being pulled inwards, of losing one's sense of self."[41] In the end one finds oneself transformed, or evolved. Getting lost in the purifying blue, which concretizes body and spirit, thus enables one to recapture an *elsewhere* that is in continual motion: "Colour is a real transformer. It changes things very directly… Recently I have tended to work more with space, with conditioning the space in such a way as to bring about different states of being. I see different works in terms of different states of being."[42] The earth is the dance floor for a wealth of I's performing the mythic dance, bearers of spirit moving according to a frantic rhythm. No two beings are alike; each has his own inimitable identity, each is a psychophysical quantum, each projects outside himself a life or body drawn from the cosmic reservoir, from the void and nothingness that surround us.

Void Field, an installation of sixteen large stones, identifies both the I and the world as they quantically occupy the same field. Between them the work finds a continuity of existence in which the distinction between organic and inorganic is false, because each is merely a different aspect of the same phenomenon. In both Western science and Eastern thought, opposites are polar; but in *Void Field*, Kapoor attempts instead to render in physical terms a field in which the I and the world move through the same space. It is a place in which the distinction between mass and void, one and many, heaven and earth, is inadmissible: "*Void Field* is a work in which this kind of binary opposition that I've always been juggling with seemed to place itself in some very clear way. It's a work about mass, about weight, about volume and then at the same time seems to be weightless, volumeless, ephemeral; it's really turning stone into sky. The darkness inside the stones is the darkness of black night, the darkness of sky."[43]

More than just a crowd of distinct individuals, *Void Field* can be seen as an urban aggregate, a segment of city modeled in stone, and made up of monuments conceived as solid domes resting on stone flooring. It is a suggestive image, transforming the sky into a solid architecture through whose openings there shines a celestial light, luminous and mysterious. And if such a thing can be conceived, then the sky can become stone: "Once I made *Void Field*, this earth into the sky, it occurred to me that it would be wonderful to attempt the opposite… In *Void Field* we have the earth containing the sky, earth outside, sky within. To do the opposite was to have earth within, sky without. I just painted some stones… And… they became bits of sky. They became weightless and in a sense effortless."[44] The work in question is *Angel*, 1989 (pp. 104–109), a series of slabs of slate covered in blue pigment and arranged freely about the floor.

Angel, a further step toward the desired union of opposites, expresses a yearning for a mutual reappropriation between heaven and earth, a step in which the purity of the immaterial becomes material. The fluidity of air is solidified, translated into the surfaces and limits of a volume. At the same time, the texture and weight of stone begin to flow, to move like a cloud or stream. The intangible becomes tangible, once again possessed in the name of the esoteric desire for absolute fusion and the reabsorption of differences. In its transmutation of energy, *Angel* is the counterpart to *Void Field*. Both deal with the transfiguration that leads to the sublime, and to the ecstasy (if not the hallucination), beyond all individual faiths, in which the celestial breath solidifies. Furthermore, *Void Field* and *Angel* represent a kind of duality. They are poles of shadow and light that imply each other, like two sides of the same coin. Together they make up a further whole, affirming that there is no such thing as a sure identity, enclosed in the comforting shell of a definition. One thing is always ready to spill over illusory into another and assume its outward appearance: "Notions about illusion are quite

Untitled, 1990

central. This is where I have a curious overlap with painting in that the space of painting is the space of illusion. I seem to be making sculpture about the space beyond, illusory space."[45]

In this dialectic between painting and sculpture, colour too assumes dual and complementary meanings. It may be affirmative and present, when laid over stone, or it may be absent and ethereal, when hidden inside stone. In terms of modern art history, the chromatic element of *Angel* and *Void Field* is an architectural crystallization of the sublime transparency that runs through painting from Barnett Newman and Mark Rothko to Yves Klein and Robert Ryman. If painters like these work on refining colour, Kapoor for his part works on petrifying it, in a kind of condensation of its astral, spiritual quality. His aim is to find the point of cohesion that will stabilize this suspended aggregate of opposites. Art serves him as the alchemic fire, purifying and regenerating so as to crystallize knowledge itself in stone. The crossing of this limit—the paradigm of light spilling over into matter— brings Kapoor's work close to the loftiest experience of holiness. It does not allow him to forget the opposition between male and female, however. Thus even at the height of his concretization of the divine—in *Angel*—he also reaffirms the power of sexual dualism, in iconographically intense, frontal works such as *Black Fire*, 1990, and *It Is Man*, 1989–90 (p. 111).

Immersion in the chasm of the body, male and female, is a way of descending in order to come back up, of plunging into the swell of flesh in order to find the light. *The Healing of St. Thomas* consists of an opening or wound of red pigment set at eye level in the wall. At the same time, however, it alludes to the doubt and redemption of Saint Thomas, realized in the transition, through a touch of the hand, from skepticism about the Resurrection to belief: "The metaphorical language is that he reaches out to touch what is apparently an illusion only to find reality. The eye and the hand need each other. Once he has touched the wound, a kind of healing takes place in Thomas. He is healed of his doubt."[46]

One could say that the juxtaposition of images (*Angel* corresponding to *Dragon*, 1992, pp. 138–41), as well as reflecting a paradigm of East and West (*Pillar of Light* corresponding to *In the Presence of the Form*, both 1991, in a dialogue between male and female), is a way for Kapoor to show that art too proceeds by antitheses and opposites. To find its light again, it must immerse itself in the flood of pure and impure, high and low, the spiritual and the sensual. So, having crystallized the heavens through colour, Kapoor achieves a further linguistic shift by trying to define light and dark without using any colour whatsoever. From the incised slab of slate in *Tomb*, 1989 (p. 113), and the vortex carved into limestone in *Oblivion*, 1994 (p. 182–83), to the

Black Fire, 1990

Three Witches, 1990

The Healing of St. Thomas, 1989-90

hollow in the floor in *Black Stones, Human Bones*, 1993 (p. 175), and the stratifications of light in *Bright Mountain*, 1993, the artist devotes himself to the experience of emptiness and fullness, darkness and light, through pure materials alone—-limestone and sandstone, sanded and polished. He wants to capture the stone's inner power, which he considers an element not of stasis but of potential action.

Limestone originates in water, a mobile, liquid element. Susceptible to evaporation, water can be transformed into air, which is itself open to further metamorphoses, one of these being fire. Kapoor's choice of limestone thus encompasses the possibility of a flux among the four elements of traditional cosmology: earth, air, fire, and water. Participating in the language of esoterism and initiation, Kapoor's limestone works reflect the perceptible processes of becoming, as they proceed, from within, from light to darkness—as we see in the seven elements of *Untitled*, 1990 (pp. 124–27), and in the great block of Kilkenny limestone in *Untitled*, 1994–95 (p. 191). Just as mud can be shaped into an endless variety of forms and images, the potential of stone is infinite, even while this medium is never amorphous. Among its possibilities is the construction of an architectonic identity through the shimmering of light, as in the great cathedrals (*Pillar of Light*, 1991). The column of light is the ideal axis linking the dwelling place to the heavens, and architecture is a metaphor of construction, as of the self. In such works as *The Healing of St. Thomas* (p. 117) and *Endless Column*, 1992 (p. 143), both the carnal and the divine, in the form of colour and stone, undergo a further transition: they find light and darkness in the components of architecture. These works openly declare their function as supports; indeed they constitute or appear in walls and ceilings. In *The Healing of St. Thomas* the bloody orifice exposes the wall's "interior space," its carnality: "The body is a building, the self is another shell . . . the idea of architecture is an image of the self."[47] In *Endless Column*, on the other hand, vaporous, fragile red pigment becomes a supporting structure, an "endless column" (Brancusi) that seems capable of passing through the entire building and up into the sky.

Just as in ancient Greek tradition the columns of Hercules marked the confines of the known world, one might say that architecture is a metaphor for approaching darkness and the unknown, a way of knowing them. In 1992, then, Kapoor "becomes" an architect. Two projects from that year— *Building for Void* (pp. 144–49) and *Descent into Limbo* (pp. 154–55)— consist of constructions, one cylindrical and one cubical, in which the interiors make historical and esoteric allusions to light and darkness, conscious and unconscious, fullness and emptiness. In assuming this role, of

The Earth, 1991

course, Kapoor always keeps in mind the mysteries and secret rituals of the temple architects, their goal being the integration of architecture into the pure cosmos of the divine.

Building for Void is a cylindrical cement edifice, fifteen metres high, designed in collaboration with David Connor for Expo '92 in Seville. From the outside it looks like a geometrical vortex about to screw itself into the ground. Inside, openings in the floor and ceiling give respectively onto darkness and light. These two moments—created below by digging a cavity into the floor and covering it in blue, and above by piercing the building's perimeter—express a death and an ascension, a stasis and a motion, the calm of the underground world and the dynamism of the heavenly.

Descent into Limbo, created for Documenta IX in Kassel, Germany, is also a concrete structure, this one six metres by six metres by six metres. If *Building for Void* posits architecture as possessing the luminosity and happy mastery of antithetical yet complementary energies, here architecture becomes dark and terrifying, due to the presence, in the centre of this great cube, of a large orifice opening onto a huge circular void, three metres in diametre. There is the illusion of a flat blue surface on the floor, but as one approaches, one realizes the sensation of standing at the edge of a precipice. The bottom is invisible, as though a fall might be infinite and eternal: Limbo. The effect creates an enormous tension, as though the earth's crust had ceased to exist and beneath it there was only an immense void, an absolute darkness.

In this dramatic ritual of entering a solid-looking concrete block, accessible only through a small door, one experiences a passage typical of the procedures of alchemy—a movement from a theatrical moment to a triumphal one. Forcing the building's opening and plunging into the space on one's way to the edge of a great void, the dark vortex of the unknown, one feels physically and psychologically alive. One has penetrated and been embraced by the magnetic force of an unknown energy. Submitting to it, one reacquires a sense of one's finitude through the experience of infinity: "The void has many presences. Its presence as fear is towards the loss of self, from a nonobject to a nonself. The idea of being somehow consumed by the object, or in the nonobject, in the body, in the cave, in the womb. I have always been drawn to a notion of fear, towards a sensation of vertigo, of falling, of being pulled inwards. This is a notion of the sublime which reverses the picture of union with light. This is an inversion, a sort of turning-inside-out. This is a vision of darkness. Fear is darkness of which the eye is uncertain, toward which the hand turns in hope of contact and in which only the imagination has the possibility of escape."[48]

The ordeal of the void, of limbo, is a necessary precondition to gaining mastery over nothingness and the self. It occurs through a dramatic experience of the breath, the unknown fearsome word, that rises up from the earth. Emptiness is at the centre of this experience, in the place where the visitor is supposed to be; while fullness is on the periphery, on the verge of engulfment in the central vortex. *Horror vacui* is transformed into invigorating, active power. The work offers yet another way to take in the vital breath of the womb of the sacred and the numinous. Finally, the infinity that yawns before one's eyes is carved out as a circle. Implying absoluteness and totality, it is a form that alludes to heaven and earth, and to all that is complete and harmonious. But the circle is also the uterus, the holy enclosure, locus of the Great Mother, primary element of creation and reproduction. Like an overturned dome, it represents the pregnant maternal womb of the earth. Inside, *Descent into Limbo* is feminine, a condition of intimate space; outside, it is masculine, a rigid, aggressive construction. House and uterus, architecture and maternity, are isomorphic; they express the meeting of the sexes.

In its Apollonian clarity, *When I Am Pregnant* (pp. 165–67), a relief swelling from the wall in an image of maternity, overcomes the ancient conflicts between the sexes to express a cohesive energy, a power capable of inaugurating life. For Kapoor, the blending of architecture and nature is above all a metaphor of the desire for a fusion of male and female. "Every man carries with him the eternal image of woman, not the image of this or that particular woman, but a definite feminine image. This image is fundamentally unconscious, an hereditary factor of primordial origin engraved in the living organic system of the man, an 'imprint' or 'archetype' of all the ancestral experiences of the female."[49] Finally, pregnancy recalls the primordial experience of movement in amniotic space, as part of a whole as yet unknown. A space of pain and joy, of frantic spasms, of severing and separation, it leads to a harrowing identity: the dawn of life.

When I Am Pregnant falls into an intermediate realm not entirely defined by either spirit or matter, for the body precedes the spirit and the spirit cannot exist independently of the body. The swelling of the wall, then, is an energetic expansion of material to ensure the existence of spirit. It is a transition between the action of the passions and the full wholeness of life. At once modest and immodest about existence, it uncovers a sweet nakedness, the nakedness of nature in her most unexpected, surprising aspect.

He who is about to be born is in a state of transition: he will literally come out on the other side. Having emerged from the void, he will exist in the

Pillar of Light, 1991

Passage, 1993

Untitled, 1994

Untitled, 1995

Untitled, 1995

pure power of fullness. He will emerge as a temporarily kindled energy in a journey between life and death, between physical and metaphysical, between conscious and unconscious, "back to proto-existence which is always surprising, always new."[50]

At the source of all birth and beginnings there is light. And Kapoor's work begins to realise the primacy of light in 1995, when the series of "Voids" — with their silent sedimentation of darkness, of the unknown, the interior, the indistinct and mysterious — are followed by works like *Turning the World Inside Out*, 1995 (pp. 206–207), and *Turning the World Upside Down*, 1995 (pp. 204–205), which return toward clarity and luminosity, toward the visible and the definite.

Here the viewer is confronted not with uncertainty, with something ungraspable, as in works from *1000 Names*, 1979–80, to *Void Field*, 1989, but with an identity like a mirror. Thus *Turning the World Inside Out* gathers its surroundings into itself, including the observer's own gaze and body. Its exterior contains and conveys a panoramic vision of the space and of the everyday life around it, even while its interior is void.

Manifesting both itself and the world outside it, this twofold being both produces and re-produces, both offers itself to our gaze and hides within that gaze, forever surrendering itself yet forever fleeing. Compared to the darkness, total yet apparently definable, of the void works from *At the Hub of Things*, 1987, to *Descent into Limbo*, 1992, the luminous *Turning the World Inside Out* defines a whole that is fleeting because it is eternally divided between interior and exterior, between hiding and reflecting, between motion and immobility. Similarly, *Turning the World Upside Down* is an ensemble in which opposites try to reconcile and meet without either contradicting each other or losing themselves in each other. Rather, they live out the vicissitudes of a dialectical existence in which the sublime coexists with the everyday, the object is affirmed in its environment, fullness is reflected in emptiness, the real lives in harmony with the abstract.

Something happens in the void, and this something eludes our grasp, for it does not really coincide with one thing or another, one space or another, one position or another. If, in the series *White Dark*, 1994–95, the correspondence between inner void and outer void makes all presence interchangeable, and affirms neither space over the other, *Turning the World Inside Out* expresses the same indefiniteness and indeterminacy of presence, in that it changes constantly, like a vortex, as it reflects light. The unexpected leap it proposes is no longer into the nothingness of darkness but into light. It gathers the secret forces of the reflective power of art, which can absorb all as well as dissolve all. To live through the experience it offers is to submit to the ordeal of loss that underlies and animates the void, embodying the enigma that every truth is born and then dies, is accessible and inaccessible, lived and created.

Capturing the force of life, as vortex, as eruption, is the essence of art, and art in turn, through the principle of opposites, triggers the reading of life. This is the alchemy of creation.

Translated from the Italian by Stephen Sartarelli

1. Gerardus van der Leeuw, *Phenomenology of Religion*, Italian trans. *Fenomenologia della religione*, Turin 1975.
2. Anish Kapoor, quoted in Constance Lewallen, "Interview with Anish Kapoor, Japan, September, 1990," «View,» vol. VII, no. 4, San Francisco 1991.
3. Kapoor, quoted in Ameena Meer, "Anish Kapoor," «Bomb,» no. 30, Winter, 1989–90, p. 38.
4. Kapoor, quoted in Lewallen, p. 5.
5. Ibid.
6. Kapoor, quoted in "Anish Kapoor interviewed by Douglas Maxwell," «Art Monthly,» London, May 1990, p. 6.
7. Ibid., p. 6.
8. Ibid., p. 7.
9. Kapoor, in an unpublished interview with Germano Celant, London, July 1995.
10. See Lynne Cooke, "Mnemic Migrations," in *Anish Kapoor*, exhibition catalogue, Oslo, Kunstnernes Hus, 1986. Cooke's essay is the first scholarly contribution to the analysis and study of the works of Kapoor between the years 1975 and 1981.
11. Kapoor, quoted in "Anish Kapoor interviewed by Douglas Maxwell," p. 9.
12. "Concerning Jung, I read books with illustrations from the complete works, like *Psychology and Alchemy*, *Alchemical Studies*, *Symbols of Transformation*." Kapoor, in the interview with Celant.
13. Kapoor, quoted in "Anish Kapoor interviewed by Douglas Maxwell," p. 7.
14. Kapoor, quoted in Lewallen, p. 5.
15. Kapoor, quoted in "Anish Kapoor interviewed by Douglas Maxwell," p. 7.
16. Kapoor, in Michael Newman, *Objects and Figures: New Sculpture in Britain*, exhibition catalogue, Edinburgh, Fruitmarket Gallery, 1982.
17. Kapoor, quoted in "Anish Kapoor interviewed by Douglas Maxwell," p. 8.
18. Ibid.
19. Kapoor, in the interview with Celant.
20. Kapoor, quoted in Marco Livingstone, *Feeling into Form*, exhibition catalogue, Liverpool, Walker Art Gallery, and Lyon, Le Nouveau Musée, 1983, p. 23.
21. Kapoor, quoted in Caroline Smulders, "*Anish Kapoor vers la dématérialisation de l'objet*," «Art Press,» no. 152,

Paris, November 1989, p. 18.
22. Kapoor, in the interview with Celant.
23. Ibid.
24. Kapoor, quoted in Livingstone, p. 15.
25. Ibid.
26. See Alessandro Rinaldi, "La ricerca della 'terza natura,'" in Marcello Fagiolo, *Natura e Artificio*, Rome, Officina Edizioni, 1979, pp. 154–175.
27. Kapoor, in the interview with Celant.
28. Ibid.
29. Ibid.
30. Kapoor, quoted in Livingstone, p. 12.
31. Ibid., p. 23.
32. Ibid., p. 27
33. Kapoor, quoted in Lewallen, p. 12.
34. Ibid., p. 16.
35. Kapoor, in the interview with Celant.
36. Kapoor, quoted in Marjorie Allthorpe-Guyton, "Mostly Hidden," in *Anish Kapoor*, exhibition catalogue, London, British Council for the XLIV Venice Biennale, 1990, p. 50.
37. Ibid., p. 45.
38. Kapoor, quoted in Lewallen, p. 16.
39. G. Tucci, *Teoria e pratica del Mandala*, Rome, Ubaldini, 1969, p. 36.
40. Kapoor, quoted in Claire Farrow, "Anish Kapoor, Theatre of Lightness, Space and Intimacy," «Art and Design,» London, no. 33, 1993, p. 53.
41. Ibid.
42. Ibid.
43. Kapoor, quoted in Lewallen, p. 21.
44. Ibid.
45. Kapoor, quoted in Allthorpe-Guyton, p. 46.
46. Kapoor, in "Homi Bhabha and Anish Kapoor. A Conversation," in *Anish Kapoor*, exhibition catalogue, Tel Aviv, Tel Aviv Museum of Art, 1993, p. 62.
47. Kapoor, in the interview with Celant.
48. Ibid.
49. C.G. Jung, *Word and Image*, Princeton, University Press, 1983, p. 226.
50. Kapoor, in "Homi Bhabha and Anish Kapoor. A Conversation," p. 60.

Works

4

10

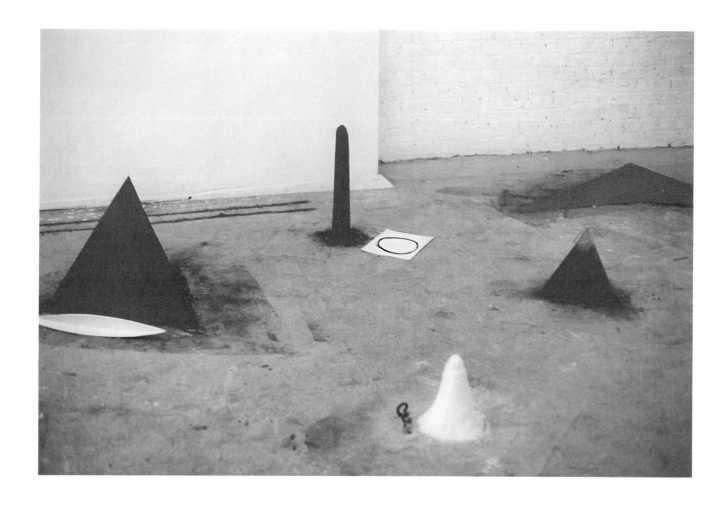

11

1000 Names, 1979-80

12

22

26

1000 Names, 1980

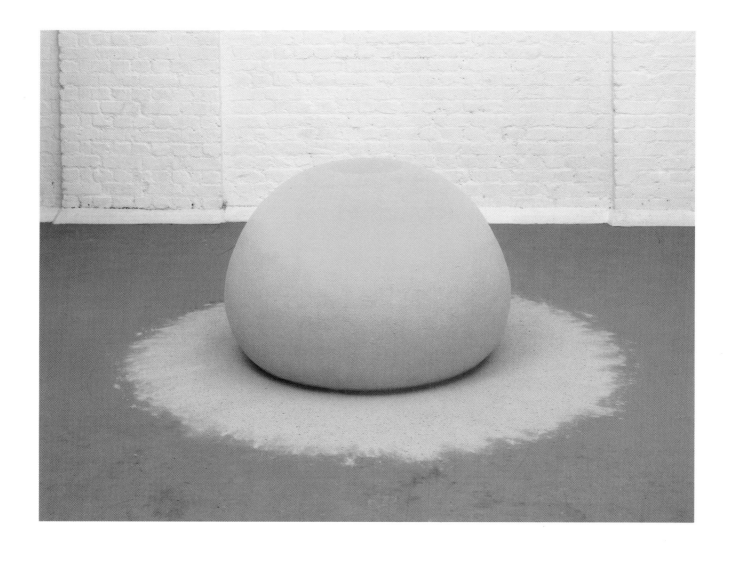

1000 Names, 1980-81

1000 Names, 1981

32

1000 Names, 1979-80

34

1000 Names, 1979-80

1000 Names, 1979-80

40

44

Part of the Red, 1981

46

Part of the Red, 1981

Part of the Red, 1981

Part of the Red, 1981

p. 50-51, 52-53
To Reflect an Intimate Part of the Red, 1981

55

As if to Celebrate I Discovered a Mountain
Blooming with Red Flowers, 1981

57

1000 Names, 1982

White Sand, Red Millet, Many Flowers, 1982

64

Untitled, 1983

70

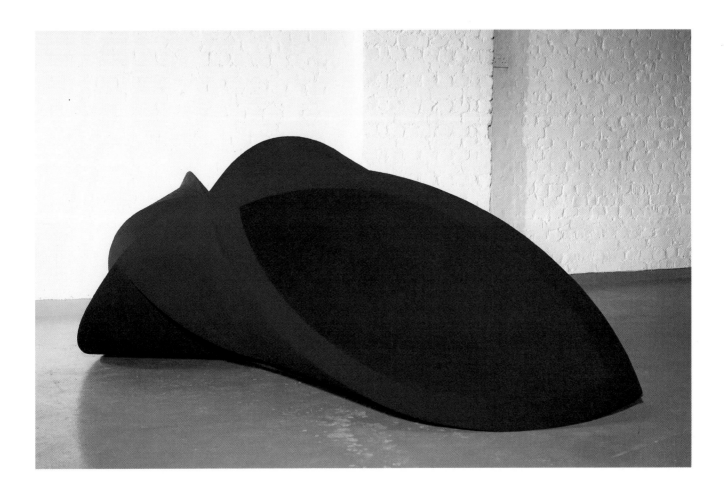

Pot for Her, 1985

72

73

Hole and Vessel II, 1984

78

Mother as a Mountain, 1985

Place, 1985

Dark, 1986

Untitled, 1986

Here and There, 1987

84

Wound, 1988

86

I, 1987

At the Hub of Things, 1987

Blood Stone, 1988

Adam, 1988-89

Adam, 1988-89

p. 94-95, 96-97
Void Field, 1989

Void Field, 1989

Void Field, 1989

102

Void Field, 1989

106

p. 104-105
Angel, 1990
It is Man, 1989

Angel, 1990
It is Man, 1989

Angel, 1990

Angel, 1990

It is Man, 1989-90

Tomb, 1989

114

Madonna, 1989-90

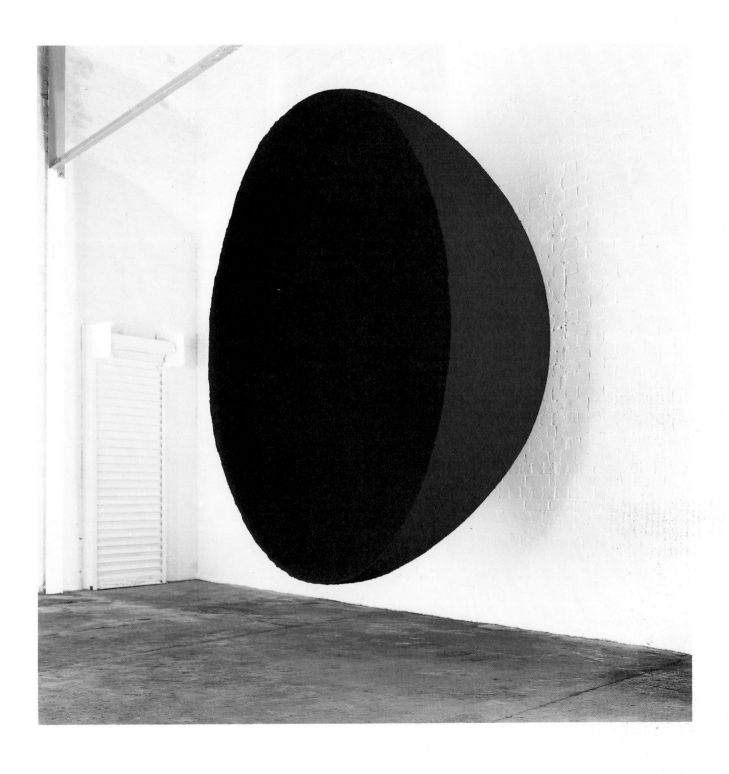

Madonna, 1989-90

The Healing of St. Thomas, 1989

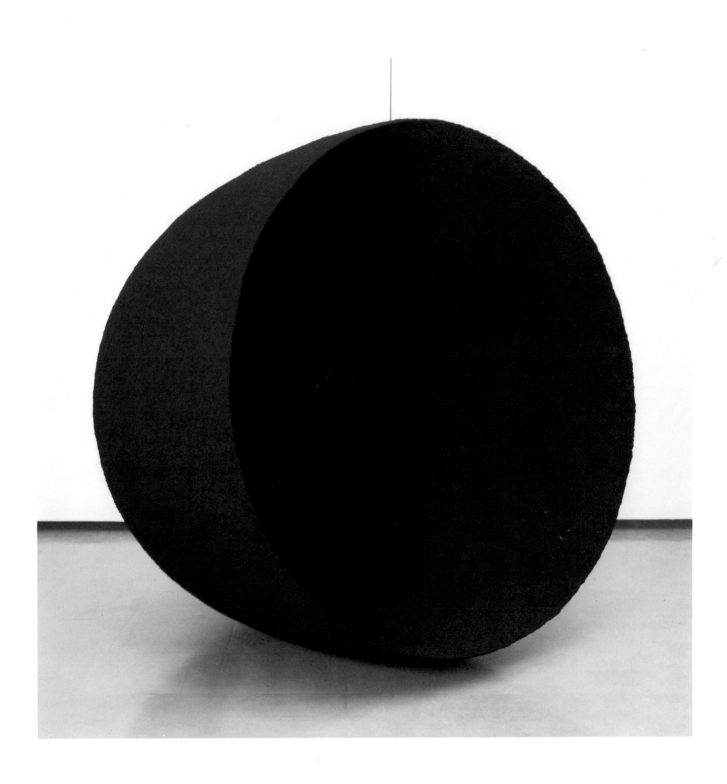

Mother as a Void, 1989-90

124

Untitled, 1990

128

p. 126-127
Untitled, 1990

Pot, 1991

130

134

136

Dragon, 1992

Dragon, 1992

142

143

Endless Column, 1992

144

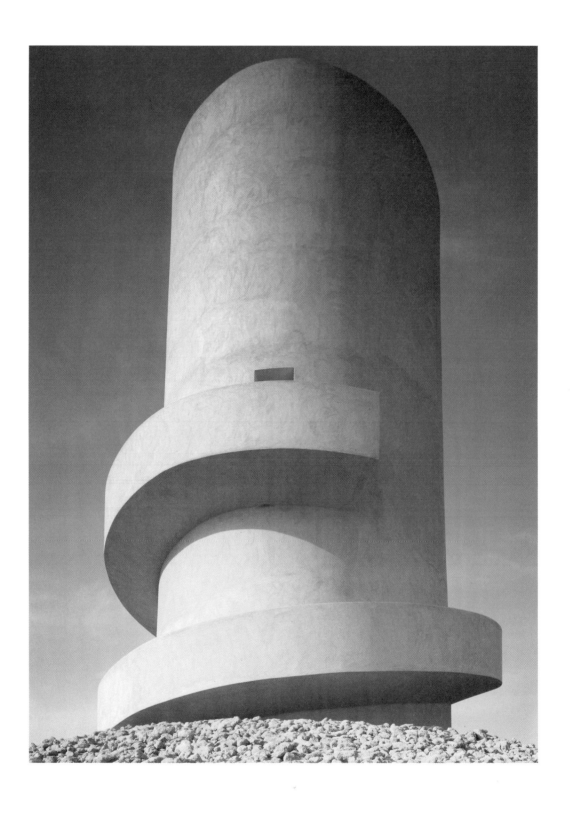

Building for a Void, 1992

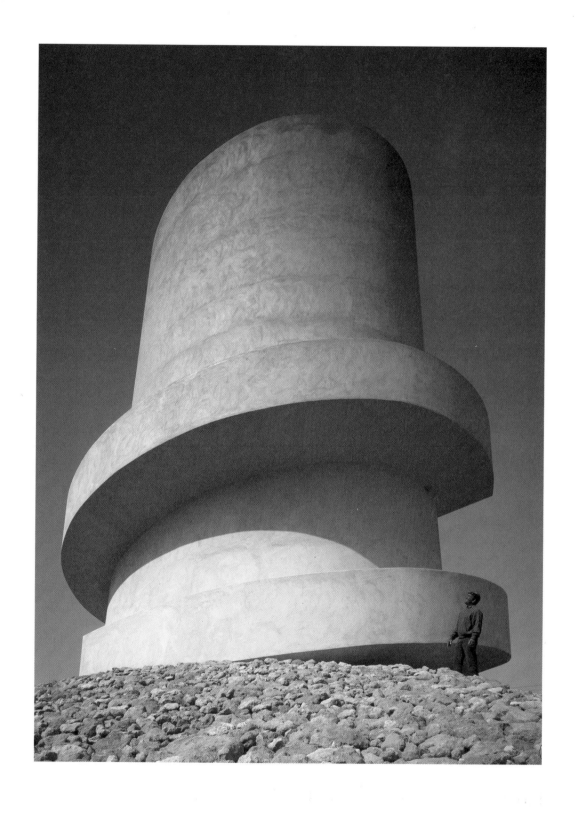

Building for a Void, 1992

Building for a Void, 1992

Building for a Void, 1992

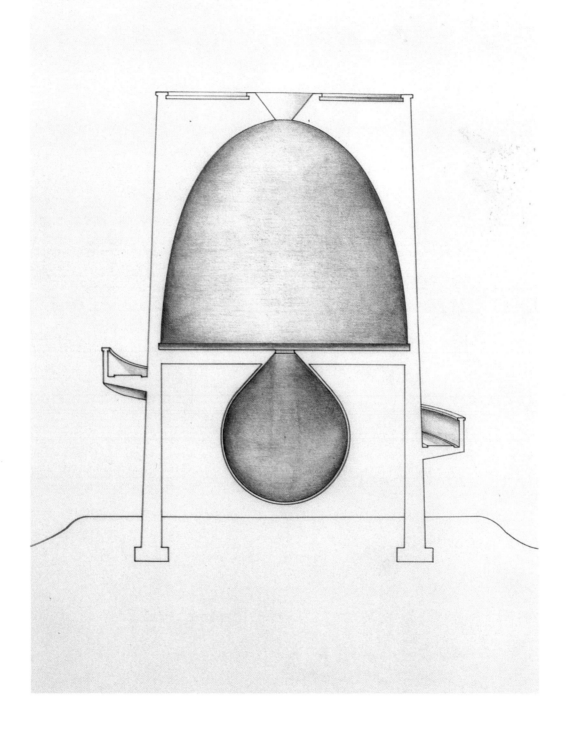

Building for a Void, 1992

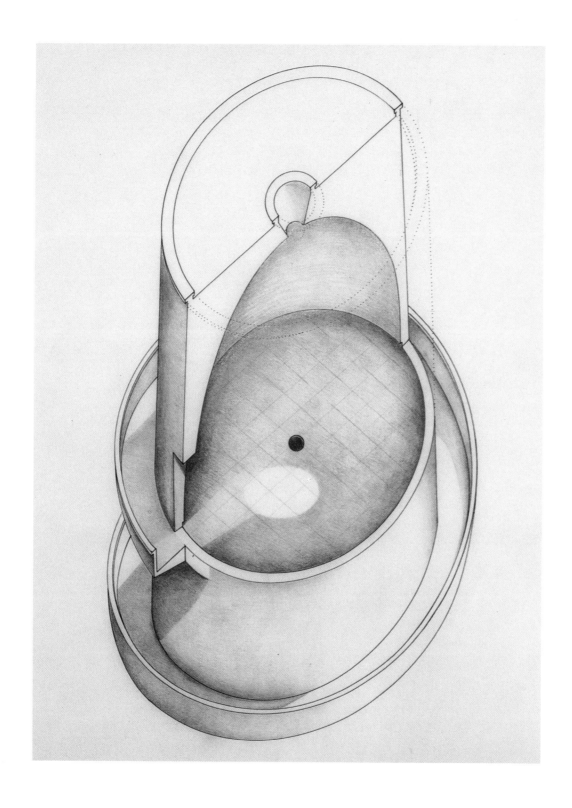

Building for a Void, 1992

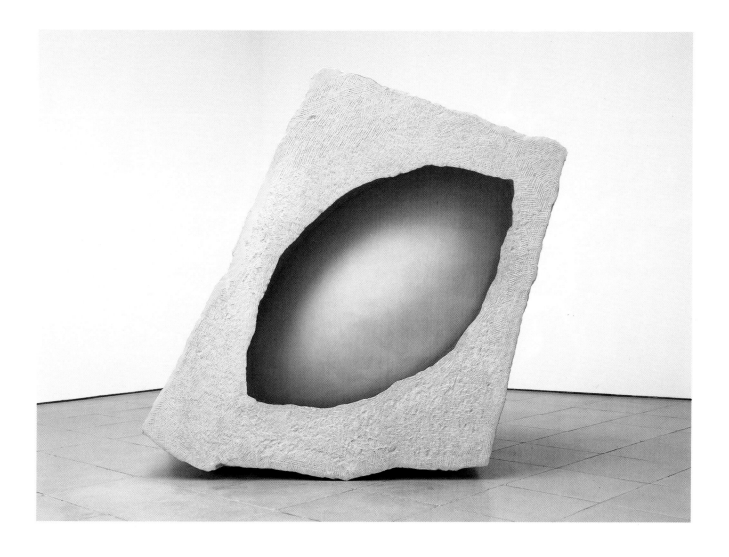

In the Presence of Form II, 1993

Untitled, 1992

154

Descent into Limbo, 1992

156

Untitled, 1993

Untitled, 1992

Untitled, 1992

When I am Pregnant, 1992

When I am Pregnant, 1992

When I am Pregnant, 1992

Untitled, 1992

169

Untitled, 1992

Untitled, 1992

171

Untitled, 1992

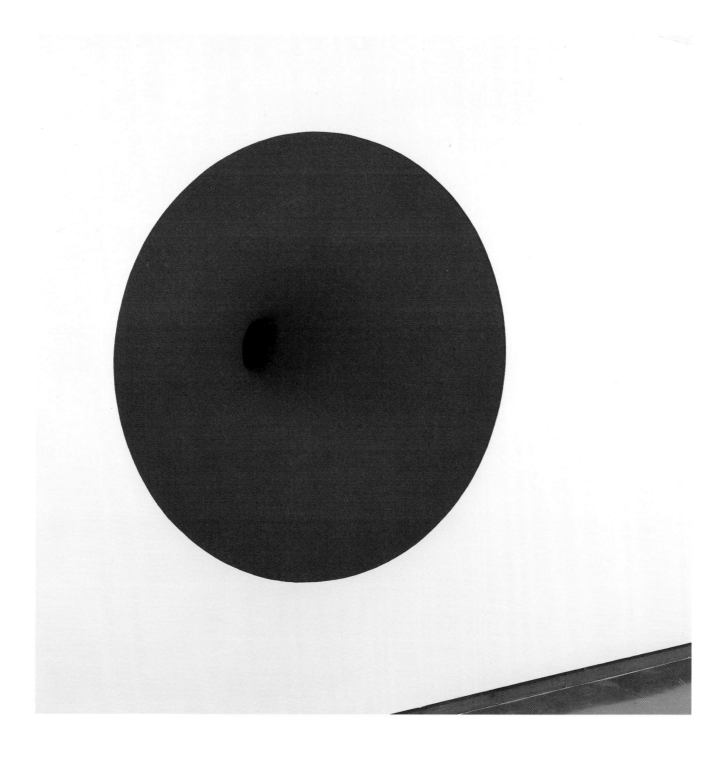

173

Untitled, 1993

Black Stones, Human Bones, 1993

178

p. 176-177
Untitled Installation, 1993

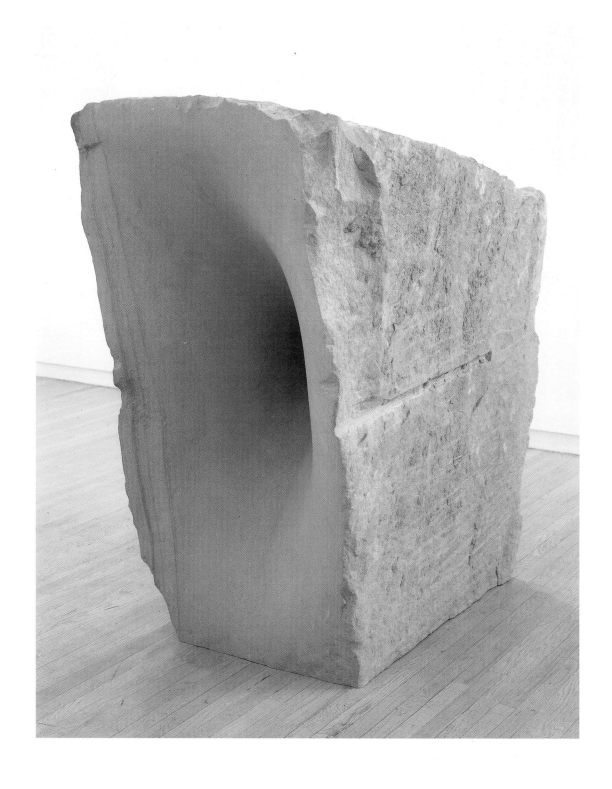

Untitled, 1993

My Body Your Body, 1993

184

p. 182-183
Oblivion, 1994

185

Oblivion, 1994

188

189

Untitled, 1994

191

Untitled, 1994-95

192

Untitled, 1995

Untitled, 1995

Untitled, 1994-95

Untitled, 1994-95

196

Untitled Installation, 1994-95

Untitled Installation, 1994-95

White Dark III, 1994-95

Untitled, 1995

Untitled, 1995

202

Mountain, 1995

203

Mountain, 1995

204

Turning the World Upside Down, 1995

208

212

List of Works

For all the images courtesy Lisson Gallery,
London

pp. 2-3
Untitled, 1977
Steel, curtain, chalk, electricity, paint

p. 5
Untitled, 1975
Paint, plaster, chalk, steel
270x120x15.2 cm

pp. 6-7
Untitled Installation, 1977-78
Silk, plaster, paint, electric motor, mixed media
900x600x450 cm

pp. 8-9, 10, 11, 13
1000 Names, 1979-80
Mixed media, pigment
Dimensions variable
Installation: studio of the artist, London

pp. 14-15, 16-17, 18-19, 20-21
1000 Names, 1979-80
Mixed media, pigment
Dimensions variable
Installation: studio of the artist, London

p. 23
1000 Names, 1980
Bonded chalk
Dimensions variable

pp. 24-25
1000 Names, 1979-80
5 elements
Mixed media, pigment
74x71.5x71.5 cm (overall)

p. 27
1000 Names, 1980
Bonded chalk
Diam 130x70 cm
Private collection, London
Installation: Starkmann Library Services,
London, 1991
Photo O. Vaering, Oslo

p. 29
1000 Names, 1980-81
Wood, gesso, pigment
102x102x102 cm
Private collection, Geneva

p. 31
1000 Names, 1981
5 elements
Mixed media, pigment
200x100x30 cm; 41x75x28 cm; 15x20x68 cm;
25x78x28 cm; 10x56x56 cm
Installation: "Prefiguration," Centre d'art
contemporain, Chambéry, 1982

p. 33
1000 Names, 1979-80
Mixed media, pigment
38x30x28 cm

p. 34
1000 Names, 1979-80
Wood, gesso, pigment
63.5x51x30.5 cm
Collection Celine and Heiner Bastian, Berlin

p. 35
1000 Names, 1979-80
Wood, chalk
50.8x38x50.8 cm

pp. 36-37, 38-39
1000 Names, 1981
5 elements
Wood, gesso, pigment
122x183x183 cm (overall)
Museo National Centro de Arte Reina Sofia,
Madrid

p. 41
1000 Names, 1979-80
Mixed media, pigment
h 183 cm ca.
Collection Sol LeWitt, Chester

pp. 42-43
1000 Names, 1979-80
Mixed media, pigment
left element: 28x91.5x91.5 cm; right:
18x91.5x91.5 cm

pp. 45, 46, 47, 49
Part of the Red, 1981
5 elements
Earth, resin, pigment
Collection Rijksmuseum Kröller-Müller, Otterlo

pp. 50-51, 52-53
To Reflect an Intimate Part of the Red, 1981
5 elements
Mixed media, pigment
200x800x800 cm (overall)
Collection of the artist, London
Photo Andrew Penketh, London

p. 55
*As if to Celebrate I Discovered a Mountain
Blooming with Red Flowers*, 1981
3 elements
Wood, cement, polystyrene, pigment
107x305x305 cm (overall)
Tate Gallery, London

p. 57
1000 Names, 1982
Earth, pigment
Stedelijk Museum, Amsterdam

p. 59
White Sand, Red Millet, Many Flowers, 1982
4 elements
Wood, cement, pigment
101x241.5x217.4 cm (overall)
Collection Arts Council, South Bank Centre,
London

pp. 60-61, 62-63
Red in the Centre, 1982
5 elements
Earth, pigment
Walker Art Gallery, Liverpool

p. 65
1000 Names, 1982
Mixed media, pigment
Private collection, Paris

p. 67
Untitled, 1983
Mixed media, pigment
120x80x20 cm
Contemporary Art Society, London

pp. 68-69
Black Earth, 1983
4 elements
Polystyrene, cement, earth, acrylic, pigment
259x271.5x236 cm (overall)

Collection Carol and Arthur Goldberg,
New York

p. 71
Pot for Her, 1985
Wood, gesso, pigment
100x275x175 cm
Private collection, Switzerland
Photo Gareth Winters, London

p. 73
Hole and Vessel II, 1984
Polystyrene, cement, earth, acrylic, pigment
95x163x109 cm
Collection G.S. Elliott, Chicago
Photo Eeva Inkeri

pp. 74-75
Six Secret Places, 1983
6 elements
Mixed media, pigment
115x425x60 cm (overall)
Collection of the artist, London
Photo Gareth Winters, London

p. 77
1000 Names, 1985
Wood, gesso, pigment
125x50x70 cm
Private collection, London
Photo Gareth Winters, London

p. 78
Mother as a Mountain, 1985
Wood, gesso, pigment
140x275x105 cm
Walker Art Center, Minneapolis, T.B. Walker
Acquisition Fund, 1987
Installation: studio of the artist
Photo Gareth Winters, London

p. 79
Place, 1985
Wood, gesso, pigment
90x80x80 cm
Private collection
Photo Gareth Winters, London

p. 80
Dark, 1986
4 elements
Wood, polystyrene, gesso, fibreglass, cloth,
pigment
25.5x25.5x53.5 cm; 66x66x94 cm;
63.5x68.5x71 cm; 305x62x77.5 cm
Allbright-Knox Museum, Buffalo

p. 81
Untitled, 1986
3 elements
Fibreglass, wood, pigment
h max 300 cm
Private collection, United States of America
Photo Sue Ormerod, London

p. 83
Here and There, 1987
Limestone, pigment
90x246.5x160 cm
Museo d'arte contemporanea Luigi Pecci,
Prato
Photo Gareth Winters, London

p. 85
Wound, 1988
Limestone, pigment
308x432x331 cm (overall)

Private collection, Zurich
Photo Susan Ormerod, London

p. 87
I, 1987
Limestone, pigment
59x63x95 cm
Collection David Michael Winton,
Minneapolis
Photo Susan Ormerod, London

p. 89
At the Hub of Things, 1987
Fibreglass, pigment
163x141x150 cm
Hirshhorn Museum and Sculpture Garden,
Washington
Photo Susan Ormerod, London

p. 91
Blood Stone, 1988
2 elements
Limestone, pigment
211x83.8x61 cm; 83.8x89x109.2 cm
Private collection, Turin
Photo Sue Ormerod, London

pp. 92, 93
Adam, 1988-89
Sandstone, pigment
119x102x236 cm
American Fund for the Tate Gallery, Courtesy
of Edwin C. Cohen (To A., A., A., and J.) on
loan to The Tate Gallery, London
Photo Larry Lame, New York

pp. 94-95, 96-97
Void Field, 1989
20 elements
Sandstone, pigment
Dimensions variable
Installation: British Pavilion, XLIV Biennale
Internazionale d'Arte, Venice, 1990
Photo Graziano Arici, Venice

p. 99
Void Field, 1989
12 elements
Sandstone, pigment
Dimensions variable
Installation: Palacio Velázquez, Parque del
Retiro, Centro de Arte Reina Sofia, Madrid, 1991
Photo Gareth Winters, London

pp. 101-103
Void Field, 1989
16 elements
Sandstone, pigment
Dimensions variable
Photo Gareth Winters, London

pp. 104-105, 107, 108, 109
Angel, 1990
11 elements
Dimensions variable

pp. 104-105, 107, 111
It is Man, 1989
Installation: Le Magasin, Centre National d'Art
Contemporain, Grenoble, 1990-91
Photo Georg Rehsteiner, Vufflens-le-Chateau

p. 108
Angel, 1990
Slate, pigment
61x264x113 cm
Photo Georg Rehsteiner, Vufflens-le-Chateau

p. 109
Angel, 1990
Slate, pigment
66x234x130 cm
Photo Georg Rehsteiner, Vufflens-le-Chateau

p. 111
It is Man, 1989-90
Sandstone, pigment
241x127x114 cm
Museo National Centro de Arte Reina Sofia,
Madrid
Photo Susan Ormerod, Gareth Winters, London

p. 113
Tomb, 1989
Slate, pigment
48.5x136x392 cm
Installation: Tel Aviv Museum of Art,
Tel Aviv, 1993
Photo Meidad Suchowolski, Tel Aviv

pp. 114, 115
Madonna, 1989-90
Fibreglass, pigment
Diam 284.5x155 cm
Museo National Centro de Arte Reina Sofia,
Madrid
Photo Susan Ormerod, Gareth Winters, London

p. 117
The Healing of St. Thomas, 1989
Mixed media
Dimensions variable
San Diego Museum of Contemporary Art,
La Jolla
Photo Georg Rehsteiner, Vufflens-le-Chateau

p. 119
Mother as a Void, 1989-90
Fibreglass, pigment
213x210x203 cm
Fukuoka Art Museum, Fukuoka

pp. 120-121
Untitled, 1990
Triptych
Fibreglass, pigment
Diam 250x167 cm each
Installation: Kunstverein, Hannover, 1991
Photo Robert Hausser, Mannheim

pp. 122-123
Three Witches, 1990
3 elements
Limestone, pigment
192x113x89 cm; 202x125x88 cm;
204x110x90 cm
National Gallery of Canada, Ottawa
Installation: Kunstverein, Hannover, 1991
Photo Robert Hausser, Mannheim

pp. 124, 125, 126-127
Untitled, 1990
7 elements
Limestone
h 125 cm ca.
Installation: Le Magasin, Centre National d'Art
Contemporain, Grenoble, 1990-91
Photo Georg Rehsteiner, Vufflens-le-Chateau

p. 129
Pot, 1991
Sandstone, pigment
Diam 152.4x156.2 cm
Installation: Kunstverein, Hannover, 1991
Photo Robert Hausser, Mannheim

p. 131
The Earth, 1991
Fibreglass, pigment
Dimensions variable
Installation: Palacio Velázquez, Parque del
Retiro, Centro de Arte Reina Sofia, Madrid, 1991
Photo Gareth Winters, London

pp. 132-133
Untitled, 1991
Marble
174x93x90 cm
Installation: Winchester Cathedral, 1995
Photo Stephen White, London

pp. 135, 137
Untitled Installation, 1991
Mixed media
Dimensions variable
The Sixth Japan Ushimado International Art
Festival, Ushimado

pp. 138-139, 140, 141
Dragon, 1992
11 elements
Sandstone, pigment
Dimensions variable
Installation: Art Tower Mito, Mito-shi, 1992-93
Photo Hirosuke Yagi, Nagoya

p. 143
Endless Column, 1992
Mixed media
Dimensions variable
Installation: San Diego Museum
of Contemporary Art, La Jolla, 1992
Photo Philipp Rittermann, San Diego

pp. 144, 145, 146, 147
Building for a Void, 1992
Project for Expo '92, Seville
In collaboration with David Connor
Concrete, stucco
h 15 m; long axis: 8 m 400 cm; short axis: 6 m
900 cm
Photo John Edward Linden, London

p. 148
Building for a Void, 1992
Project for Expo '92, Seville
In collaboration with David Connor
Axonometry, Section BB
Rendering by Nicholas Alderson

p. 149
Building for a Void, 1992
Project for Expo '92, Seville
In collaboration with David Connor
Axonometry
Rendering by Nicholas Alderson

p. 151
In the Presence of Form II, 1993
Portland stone
175x201x122 cm
Heide Park and Art Gallery, Victoria, Australia
Photo Stephen White, London

p. 153
Untitled, 1992
Mixed media
Dimensions variable

p. 154, 155
Descent into Limbo, 1992
Project for Documenta IX, Kassel, 1992
Concrete, stucco

216

6x6x6 m
Photo Dirk De Neef, Gent

p. 157
Untitled, 1993
Plaster, pigment
189.5x76.5x166 cm
Photo Stephen White, London

pp. 158-159
Eyes Turned Inward, 1993
2 elements
Fibreglass, pigment
155x155x135.5 cm (overall)
Collection Fundacion Berardo, Lisbona
Installation: Tel Aviv Museum of Art, 1993
Photo Meidad Suchowolski, Tel Aviv

p. 160
Entrances to *Untitled*, 1992
(p. 161) and *Untitled*, 1992 (p. 163)
Installation: "De Opening," De Pont
Foundation for Contemporary Art, Tilburg,
1992

pp. 160, 161
Untitled, 1992
Fibreglass, acrylic, pigment
Diam 100 cm
Photo Hans Biezen

p. 163
Untitled, 1992
Polystyrene, aluminium, fibreglass, acrylic,
pigment
Dimensions variable, diam 220 cm
De Pont Foundation for Contemporary Art,
Tilburg
Photo Hans Biezen

p. 165, 166, 167
When I am Pregnant, 1992
Mixed media
Dimensions variable
De Pont Foundation for Contemporary Art,
Tilburg
Installation: De Pont Foundation for
Contemporary Art, Tilburg, 1995

p. 168, 169, 170
Untitled, 1992
Sandstone, pigment
241x150x119 cm
Collection Fondazione Prada, Milan

pp. 168, 170, 171
Untitled, 1992
Sandstone, pigment
230x122x103 cm
Installation: De Pont Foundation
for Contemporary Art, Tilburg, 1995

p. 173
Untitled, 1993
Fibreglass, pigment
Photo Dan Barsotti

p. 175
Black Stones, Human Bones, 1993
2 elements
Marble
131x163x171.5 cm; diam 90 cm
Installation: "The Siege," Obidos, 1993
Photo Jose Manuel Costa Alves

pp. 176-177
Untitled Installation, 1993
Dimensions variable
Installation: Barbara Gladstone Gallery,
New York, 1993-94

p. 179
Untitled, 1993
Sandstone
165x92x145 cm
Installation: Barbara Gladstone Gallery,
New York, 1993-94

p. 181
My Body Your Body, 1993
Fibreglass, pigment
Dimensions variable; element: 248x103x205 cm
Photo Attilio Maranzano, Rome

pp. 182-183
Oblivion, 1994
Limestone
142x98x114 cm; 142x98x145 cm;
122x132x122 cm
Installation: "Asian Art Now," Hiroshima City
Museum of Contemporary Art, Hiroshima,
1994

p. 185
Oblivion, 1994
Limestone
142x98x145 cm
Installation: "Asian Art Now," Hiroshima City
Museum of Contemporary Art, Hiroshima, 1994

pp. 186-187
Mountain, 1994
Cast iron
285x420x210 cm
Commission: Municipality of Tachikawa, Japan
Photo Anzai

p. 188
Untitled, 1994
Fibreboard, paint
89x120x241 cm
Vancouver Art Gallery, Vancouver
Photo Andrew Penketh, London

p. 189
Untitled, 1994
Fibreboard, paint
156.6x125x248 cm
Private collection, Turin
Photo Andrew Penketh, London

p. 191
Untitled, 1994-95
Kilkenny limestone
202.5x140x125 cm
De Pont Foundation for Contemporary Art,
Tilburg
Installation: De Pont Foundation for
Contemporary Art, Tilburg, 1995

pp. 192, 193
Untitled, 1995
Aluminium
149x98x99 cm
Installation: De Pont Foundation for
Contemporary Art, Tilburg, 1995

pp. 194, 195
Untitled, 1994-95
Limestone
188x150x175 cm
Installation: De Pont Foundation for
Contemporary Art, Tilburg, 1995

pp. 196, 197
Untitled Installation, 1994-95
Wood, paint
206x152.6x127.8 cm; 206x152.3x127.2 cm
Installation: De Pont Foundation for
Contemporary Art, Tilburg, 1995

p. 198
White Dark III, 1994-95
Wood, fibreglass, paint
206x152.6x127.8 cm
Photo John Riddy, London

p. 199
Untitled, 1995
2 elements
Gourds, acrylic pigment
25.5x26.5x71.5 cm
Photo Stephen White, London

p. 200
Untitled, 1995
Gourds
32x140x115 cm
Installation: Lisson Gallery, London, 1995
Photo John Riddy, London

p. 201
Untitled, 1995
Gourds, pigment
55x67x32 cm
Installation: Lisson Gallery, London, 1995
Collection Fondazione Prada, Milan

pp. 202, 203
Mountain, 1995
Fibreboard, paint
317.5x249x404.5 cm
Private collection, Brussels
Installation: Lisson Gallery, London, 1995
Photo John Riddy, London

pp. 204, 205
Turning the World Upside Down, 1995
Stainless steel
120x120x120 cm
Installation: Fondazione Prada, Milan, 1995

pp. 206-207
Turning the World Inside Out, 1995
Cast aluminium
148x184x188 cm
Photo John Riddy, London

p. 209
Cloud, 1995
Wood, fibreglass, paint
205.7x152.4x126.9 cm
Installation: Fondazione Prada, Milan, 1995

pp. 210-211, 213
Turning the World Inside Out II, 1995
Chromium-plated bronze
145x185x185 cm
Installation: Fondazione Prada, Milan, 1995

217

Biography

1954	Born Bombay, India
1973-77	Hornsey College of Art, London
1977-78	Chelsea School of Art, London
1979	Taught at Wolverhampton Polytechnic
1982	Artist-in-Residence, Walker Art Gallery, Liverpool
1990	Premio Duemila at the Venice Biennale
1991	Turner Prize
	Lives and works in London

Exhibition History

Information regarding *Solo Exhibitions* listed
in sequence, according to city, exhibition site,
title of exhibition, length of exhibition, data
provided in catalogue (if one exists; for
complete information on catalogues see
bibliography, section *Books, Solo Exhibitions
Catalogues*) and in texts contained therein.
There follows a complete list of exhibited
works and a selection of the most important
reviews.
Information regarding the title, date, technique
and size (height, width, depth in cms.)
is supplied for each piece listed.
The measurements of works comprising
different elements indicate overall size, unless
otherwise specified. Pieces featured in more
than one exhibition are described in detail only
for the first exhibition; afterwards, they are
accompanied by a brief description and an
asterisk.
For *Group Exhibitions*, the criterion and the
sequence according to which information is
supplied is the same, but only the titles of
works created for a particular exhibition
appear in the square brackets.

Solo Exhibitions

1980
Paris, Patrice Alexandre.
Works in exhibition: *1000 Names*, 1979–80, five elements, mixed media, pigment, 74x71.5x71.5 cm; *1000 Names*, 1979–80, mixed media, pigment, 35.5x22.9x33 cm; *1000 Names*, 1979–80, two elements, mixed media, pigment, 28x200x91.5 cm.

1981
London, Coracle Press, 3 April–1 May.
Works in exhibition: *1000 Names*, 1979–80* [Alexandre 1980, two elements]; *1000 Names*, 1981, mixed media, chalk, 70x130 cm; *1000 Names*, 1981, five elements, wood, chalk, pigment, 122x183x183 cm.

1982
Liverpool, Walker Art Gallery, 13 March–18 April.
Works in exhibition: *As if to Celebrate I Discovered a Mountain Blooming with Red Flowers*, 1981, five elements, wood, cement, polystyrene, pigment, 107x305x305 cm.

London, Lisson Gallery, 19 May–12 June.
Works in exhibition: *White Sand, Red Millet, Many Flowers*, 1982, four elements, wood, cement, pigment, 101x241.5x217.4 cm; *Red in the Centre*, 1982, earth, pigment, dimensions variable; *Red in the Centre II*, 1982, earth, pigment, dimensions variable; *1000 Names*, 1982, earth, pigment; six untitled drawings, mixed media on paper.
- William Feaver, "Charred remains," «The Observer,» London, 30 May 1982;
- Caroline Collier, "Anish Kapoor," «Arts Review,» London, 4 June 1982, pp. 289–290;
- Michael Newman, "Anish Kapoor," "Art Monthly," no. 58, London, July–Aug. 1982, p. 15;
- John Coleman, "Anish Kapoor, Lisson Gallery," «Flash Art International,» no. 110, Milan, 1983.

1983
Rotterdam, Galerie 't Venster, 21 Jan.–23 Feb. (organized by The Rotterdam Arts Council). Catalogue with text by Michael Newman.
Works in exhibition: *1000 Names*, 1980; *1000 Names*, 1980; *1000 Names*, 1980; *To Reflect an Intimate Part of the Red*, 1981, five elements, mixed media, pigment, 200x800x800 cm ca.; *As if to Celebrate I Discovered a Mountain Blooming with Red Flowers*, 1981*; *1000 Names*, 1982; *Three*, 1982, four elements, wood, cement, earth, pigment, 91.5x91.5x91.5 cm ca. each; *1000 Names*, 1982; *1000 Names*, 1982.
- Paul Groot, "Anish Kapoor: 't Venster Gallery," «Flash Art International,» no. 112, Milan, May 1983, pp. 70–71.

Liverpool, Walker Art Gallery, "Feeling into Form," 16 March–17 April. Catalogue with text by Marco Livingstone. Traveled to Villeurbanne, Lyon, Le Nouveau Musée, 20 May–5 July.
Works in exhibition: *1000 Names*, 1981, two elements, wood, cement, polystyrene, pigment, 30x30x30 cm ca. each; *Three*, 1982*; *Red in the Centre*, 1982, five elements, earth, pigment; *Tongue*, 1982, wood, cement, polystyrene, pigment, 61x91.5x91.5 cm ca. each; *Full*, 1983, five elements, wood, cement, polystyrene, pigment, four elements 91.5x91.5x91.5 cm ca., one element 107x61x107 cm ca.; *Six Secret Places*, 1983, mixed media, pigment, 115x425x60 cm; *1000 Names*, 1983, wood, cement, polystyrene, pigment, 107x107x107 cm ca.; *1000 Names*, 1983, two elements, wood, cement, polystyrene, pigment.

London, Lisson Gallery, 22 Oct.–19 Nov.
Works in exhibition: *Untitled*, 1983, mixed media, gold leaf, 70x70x70 cm; *1000 Names*, 1983, mixed media, 38x38x38 cm; *1000 Names*, 1983, mixed media, gold leaf, 45x55x31 cm; *1000 Names*, 1983, mixed media, 120x80x20 cm; *1000 Names*, 1983, mixed media, 35x30x48 cm; *Hole and Vessel*, 1983, mixed media, pigment, 240x150x60 cm; *1000 Names*, 1983, mixed media, 45x30x45 cm; *1000 Names*, 1983, mixed media, 55x18x45; *Six Secret Places*, 1983, mixed media, 115x425x60 cm; *1000 Names*, 1983, mixed media, 50x50x60 cm; *Untitled*, 1983, mixed media, 70x70x70 cm; *1000 Names*, 1983, mixed media, 39x39x39 cm.
- Amanda Baillieu, "Strange Monoliths," «LAM Magazines,» Oct. 1983;
- Sarah Kent, "Review," «Time Out,» London, 3–9 Nov. 1983;
- Richard Cork, "Lucid Form," «Evening Standard,» London, 3 Nov. 1983;
- Mary Rose Beaumont, "Anish Kapoor, Lisson Gallery," «Arts Review,» London, 11 Nov. 1983;
- Caroline Collier, "Anish Kapoor at the Lisson Gallery," «Studio International,» no. 1003, Dec. 1983, p. 51;
- John Coleman, "Anish Kapoor, Lisson Gallery," «Flash Art,» no. 115, Milan, Jan. 1984, p. 39.

1984
New York, Barbara Gladstone Gallery, 3–31 March.
Works in exhibition: *Black Earth*, 1983, four elements, polystyrene, cement, earth, acrylic, pigment, 259x571.5x236 cm; *Chant of Blue*, 1984, three elements, polystyrene, cement, earth, acrylic, pigment, 129.5x272x213.5 cm; *Half*, 1984, polystyrene, cement, earth, pigment, diam 170x96.5 cm; *1000 Names*, 1984, polystyrene, cement, earth, pigment, 70x70x84 cm; *1000 Names*, 1984, polystyrene, cement, earth, pigment, 33x30.5x84 cm; *Half*, 1984, polystyrene, cement, earth, pigment, 86.3x104x45.7 cm; *Untitled*, 1984, polystyrene, cement, pigment, 101.6x106.6x137.2 cm; *1000 Names*, 1984, polystyrene, earth, cement, wood, pigment, 40.6x38x35.3 cm; *Hole and Vessel*, 1984, polystyrene, cement, earth, pigment, 92.2x162.2x110 cm.
- Dan Cameron, "Anish Kapoor," «Arts Magazine,» March 1984, p. 4;
- John Russell, "Anish Kapoor," «The New York Times, Weekend Section,» New York, 23 March 1984;
- D.J., "Anish Kapoor," «Currents,» no. 39, New York, April 1984;
- Ellen Handy, "Anish Kapoor," «Arts Magazine,» May 1984, p. 44;
- Nancy Princenthal, "Anish Kapoor, Barbara Gladstone," «Artnews,» New York, Summer 1984, p. 189;
- Kenneth Baker, "Anish Kapoor at Barbara Gladstone," «Art in America,» no. 72, New York, Oct. 1984, pp. 189–190.

1985
London, Lisson Gallery, 4–23 Sept.

Places, 1983, mixed media, pigment, 115x425x60 cm; *1000 Names*, 1983, wood, cement, polystyrene, pigment, 107x107x107 cm ca.; *1000 Names*, 1983, two elements, wood, cement, polystyrene, pigment.

Works in exhibition: *In Search of the Mountain II*, 1985, wood, chalk, pigment, 100x45x65 cm; *Pot for Her*, 1985, wood, chalk, pigment, 100x275x175 cm; *1000 Names*, 1985, wood, chalk, pigment 125x50x70 cm; *Mother as a Mountain*, 1985, wood, chalk, pigment, 145x200x145 cm; *Place*, 1985, wood, chalk, pigment, 90x80x80 cm; *The Pot is a God I*, 1985, wood, chalk, pigment, 45x80x80 cm; *The Pot is a God II*, 1985, wood, chalk, pigment, 55x45x40 cm; three untitled drawings, 1985, mixed media on paper.
- Sarah Kent, "Anish Kapoor," «Time Out,» London, 19–25 Sept. 1985;
- Caroline Collier, "Forms a hole can take...: Anish Kapoor, London, Lisson Gallery," «Studio International,» Vol. 198, no. 1010, pp. 43–44;
- Marina Vaizey, "A new star carves out a sculpture for our time," «The Sunday Times,» London, 8 Sept. 1985;
- William Packer, "The age of discardment," «Financial Times,» New York, 19 Sept. 1985.

Basel, Kunsthalle, 6 Oct.–10 Nov. Catalogue with texts by Jean-Christophe Ammann, Alexander von Grevenstein, Ananda Coomaraswamy. Traveled to Eindhoven, Stedelijk Van Abbemuseum, 3 May–8 June 1986.
Works in exhibition: *To Reflect an Intimate Part of the Red*, 1981*; *Six Secret Places*, 1983*; *Untitled*, 1983, mixed media, h 152 cm ca.; *Untitled*, 1985, mixed media, 254x114.5x114.5 cm; *In Search of the Mountain II*, 1985*; *Pot for Her*, 1985*; *1000 Names*, 1985*; *Mother as Mountain*, 1985*; *Place*, 1985, mixed media, 90x80x80 cm; *The Pot is a God I*, 1985*; *The Pot is a God II*, 1985*; six untitled drawings, 1985, mixed media on paper.
- Siegmar Gassert, "Tisch und Stuhl und Kreis und Kugel und Muschel," «Basler Zeitung,» Basel, 7 Oct. 1985;
- "'Noli me tangere' und 'Beruhren gestattet'," «Basellandschaftliche Zeitung,» Liestal, Switzerland, 9 Oct. 1985;
- P.B., "Neues aus Amerika und Indien," «Der Bund,» Bern, 10 Oct. 1985;
- Roman Hollenstein, "Von Johns und Artschwager bis Kapoor," «Neue Zurcher Zeitung,» Zurich, 10 Oct. 1985;
- Susan Moser–Ehinger, "Auf den Skulpturen liegt leuchtend farbiges Pulver," «Südkurier Konstanz,» Konstanz, Germany, 11 Oct. 1985;
- Susan Moser–Ehinger, "Zum Berühren und Nichtberühren," «Solothurner Zeitung,» Solothurn, Switzerland, 12 Oct. 1985;
- Max Wechsler, "Werke Richard Artschwager und Anish Kapoor," «Vaterland,» Luzern, 16 Oct. 1985;
RD., "Der lange und der endlose Weg," «Nordschweiz,» Basel, 16 Oct. 1985;
- Anneliese Zwez, "Zwei Pole: Intellektuelle Konzepte un sinnliche Strahlkraft," «Aargauer Tagblatt,» Aargau, Switzerland, 17 Oct. 1985;
- Guy Curdy, "Illusion et Couleur," «Le Démocrate,» Delémont, Switzerland, 19 Oct. 1985;
- Philippe Mathonnet, "Poudre aux yeux et faux bois!," «Journal de Genève,» Geneva, 19 Oct. 1985;
- "Faszination der Gegensätze," «Basler Az.,» Basel, 25 Oct. 1985;
- "Das Kunstwerk als Wahrnehmungsgegenstand," «Bünder Zeitung,» Chur, Switzerland, 7 Nov. 1985.

Studio of the artist, London, 1983

Kunsthalle Basel, Basel, 1985

Kunsthalle Basel, Basel, 1985

Lisson Gallery, London, 1988

Barbara Gladstone Gallery, New York, 1989

Kohji Ogura Gallery, Nagoya, 1989

British Pavilion, XLIV Biennale Internazionale d'Arte, Venice, 1990

1986

Oslo, Kunstnernes Hus. Catalogue with texts by Arne Malmedal and Lynne Cooke.
Works in exhibition: *1000 Names*, 1981* [Coracle Press 1981, 70x130 cm]; *To Reflect an Intimate Part of the Red*, 1981*; *Place*, 1985*; *1000 Names*, 1981, five elements, mixed media, dimensions variable.

New York, Barbara Gladstone Gallery, 3–31 May.
Works in exhibition: *Untitled*, 1986, polystyrene, chalk, cloth, pigment, 75x75x45.7 cm; *Untitled*, 1986, polystyrene, chalk, cloth, pigment, 73.5x73.5x61 cm; *Dark*, 1986, polystyrene, chalk, fibreglass, cloth, pigment, 305x317.5x266 cm circa; *A Flower, a Drama like Death*, 1986, three elements, polystyrene, chalk, cloth, pigment, 56x355x152.5 cm; *Untitled*, 1986, wood, cloth, chalk, pigment, 123.2x123.2x66 cm; *Place*, 1985*; *Blue Flower*, 1986, polystyrene, cloth, chalk, pigment, 50.8x50.8x50.8 cm.
- John Russell, "Bright Young Talents: Six Artists with a Future," «The New York Times,» Section 2, New York, 18 May 1986, pp. 1, 31;
- "Anish Kapoor, Barbara Gladstone," «Artforum,» New York, Nov. 1986.

Amherst, University Gallery, Fine Arts Center, University of Massachusetts, "Anish Kapoor: Recent Sculpture and Drawings," 1 Nov.–14 Dec. Catalogue with text by Helaine Posner.
Works in exhibition: *1000 Names*, 1980, wood, chalk, pigment, 53.5x10x37 cm; *Black Earth*, 1983*; *Hole and Vessel*, 1984*; *Place*, 1985*; *Blue Flower*, 1986*; *A Flower, a Drama like Death*, 1986*; seven untitled drawings, 1984–86, mixed media on paper.

1987

Sydney, Ray Hughes Gallery, "Anish Kapoor: on Paper 1975–1987." Catalogue with interview by Richard Cork. Traveled to Brisbane, Museum of Modern Art.
Works in exhibition: seventy-nine untitled drawings, 1975–87, mixed media on paper.

1988

London, Lisson Gallery, 11 April–7 May.
Works in exhibition: *Painting No. 1*, 1986, earth, oil, pigment on wood, 177x122 cm; *Painting No. 2*, 1987, earth, oil, papier mâché on wood, 178x122 cm; *Painting No. 3*, 1987, sawdust, earth, acrylic on wood, 177x122 cm; *At the Hub of Things*, 1987, fibreglass, pigment, 163x141 cm, diam 150 cm; *Virgin*, 1987–88, microcrystalline wax, fibreglass, pigment, h 110 cm, diam 168 cm; *Body*, 1988, microcrystalline wax, mixed media, h 110 cm, diam 173 cm; *I*, 1987, limestone, 59x63x95 cm; *Wound*, 1988, limestone, pigment, 308x432x331 cm; *Sky*, 1988, earth, mixed media, 48x206x122 cm.
- Marina Vaizey, "Shaping up to Abstracts," «The Sunday Times,» London, 17 April 1988;
- David Lee, "Anish Kapoor, Lisson Gallery," «Arts Review,» London, 22 April 1988;
- Rupert Martin, "The Journey from an Earthly to a Heavenly Body," «Flash Art International,» Milan, Summer 1988, p. 159.

1989

New York, Barbara Gladstone Gallery, 1–29 April.

Works in exhibition: *Adam*, 1988–89, sandstone, pigment, 120.6x104x238.5 cm; *Void*, 1988–89, fibreglass, pigment, 205.5x205.5x115.5 cm; *Untitled*, 1989, limestone, pigment, 194.5x200.5x77.5 cm; *Moonstone*, 1989, slate, pigment, 129.5x105.5x37 cm.
- Peter Schjeldahl, "Earthy but Housebroken," «7 Days,» New York, 19 April 1989;
- Eleanor Heartney, "Anish Kapoor," «Tema Celeste,» English edition, no. 21, July–Sept. 1989;
- Stephen Westfall, "Anish Kapoor, Barbara Gladstone Gallery," «Flash Art,» no. 147, Summer 1989;
- "Anish Kapoor, Barbara Galdstone Gallery," «Arts Magazine,» Sept. 1989, p. 98;
- «Arts Magazine,» Oct. 1989, p. 46.

Nagoya, Japan, Kohji Ogura Gallery, 9 Sept.–14 Oct. (in collaboration with Lisson Gallery, London). Catalogue with text by Pier Luigi Tazzi.
Works in exhibition: *Virgin*, 1987–88*; *Void*, 1989, fibreglass, pigment, 121.9x121.9x91.4 cm; *Mother as a Ship*, 1989, fibreglass, pigment, 215.9x119.3x106.6 cm; *1000 Names*, 1979–80, wood, chalk, 76x76x38 cm.

London, Lisson Gallery, "Void Field," 1 Dec.–4 Jan. 1990.
Works in exhibition: *Void Field*, 1989, sixteen elements, sandstone, pigment, dimensions variable; *Angel*, 1989, slate, pigment, 245x150x42 cm.
- Andrew Graham–Dixon, "Pride and Prejudice," «The Independent,» London, 5 Dec. 1989;
- Richard Dorment, "Vexed questions of colour," «Daily Telegraph,» London, 9 Dec. 1989;
- William Feaver, "Voices from the void," «The Observer,» London, 10 Dec. 1989, p. 44;
- Marina Vaizey, "Why elementsality does not tell the whole story," «The Sunday Times,» London, 10 Dec. 1989;
- William Packer, "Sculptor with the best of both worlds," «Financial Times,» London, 12 Dec. 1989;
- Sarah Kent, "Anish Kapoor," «Time Out,» London, 13 Dec. 1989;
- Richard Cork, "Airy as a rock," «The Listener,» London, 14 Dec. 1989, p. 42;
- David Lillington, "Anish Kapoor," «Arts Review,» Vol. 41, no. 25, London, 15 Dec. 1989, pp. 889–890;
- Giles Auty, "Anish Kapoor at Lisson Gallery," «Spectator,» London, 16 Dec. 1989, p. 35;
- Mark Currah, "Anish Kapoor, Lisson Gallery," «City Limits,» London, 21 Dec. 1989, p. 109;
- Noemi Smolik, "Anish Kapoor, Lisson, London," «Noema,» Jan. 1989–Feb. 1990, p. 66–67;
- Andrew Renton, "Art," «Blitz,» London, 1 Feb. 1990, p. 28;
- Marjorie Allthorpe–Guyton, "Anish Kapoor, Lisson Gallery," «Artforum,» New York, March 1990, pp. 175–176;
- Andrew Renton, "Anish Kapoor, Lisson," «Flash Art International,» Milan, no. 151, March–April 1990, pp. 151–152;
- William Feaver, "Anish Kapoor," «Artnews,» New York, April 1990, p. 179.

1990

Venice, Giardini di Castello, English Pavilion, XLIV Biennale Internazionale d'Arte, "Anish Kapoor," 27 May–30 Sept. (organized by British Council). Catalogue with texts by Thomas McEvilley and Marjorie Allthorpe–Guyton.
Works in exhibition: *The Healing of St. Thomas*, 1989, mixed media, dimensions variable; *Void Field*, 1989*; *It Is Man*, 1989–90, sandstone, pigment, 241x127x114 cm; *Madonna*, 1989–90, fibreglass, pigment, diam 284.5x155 cm; *Black Fire*, 1990, fibreglass, pigment, anthracite, 315x508x180 cm; *A Wing at the Heart of Things*, 1990, two elements, slate, pigment, 28x353x270 cm, 25x295x320 cm.
- "XLIV Venice Biennale 1990," «Visual Arts News,» no. 31, Jan. 1990, p. 1;
- Marjorie Allthorpe–Guyton, "Original sites. The sculpture of Anish Kapoor," «Artscribe,» May 1990, pp. 50–52;
- Penelope Curtis, "Sculpture on the threshold," «The Antique Collector,» May 1990, pp. 66–73;
- Sarah Kent, "Mind over matter," «20/20,» no. 14, May 1990, pp. 36–40;
- Louisa Buck, "Pigments of the imagination," «Sunday Correspondent,» London, 13 May 1990, pp. 10–14;
- Ann Hindry, "Champs de pierre d'Anish Kapoor," «Beaux Arts,» June 1990, pp. 64–77;
- Lisa Licitra Ponti, "Journey to Venice," «l'Arca,» July–Aug. 1990;
- John Kemp, "Stones of Venice: Anish Kapoor at the Biennale," «Modern Painters,» Vol. 3, no. 2, Summer 1990, pp. 44–46;
- Doris Van Drateln, "Anish Kapoor, Ein Gespräch," «Kunstforum,» Vol. 109, Aug.–Oct. 1990, pp. 304–315;
- Bojana Pejic, "What will become of our sensitive skin...," «Artforum,» Vol. XXIX, no. 1, New York, Sept. 1990, pp. 130–132;
- Domenico Scudero, "XLIV Venice Biennale," «Tema Celeste,» Syracuse, Nov.–Dec. 1990.

New York, Barbara Gladstone Gallery, "Drawings," 18 Sept.–6 Oct.
Works in exhibition: twenty-one untitled drawings, 1987–90, mixed media on paper.
- Gregory Galligan, "Steamed-up mirrors and boogie-woogies," «Art International,» no. 14, Spring–Summer 1990;
- Michael Brenson, "Anish Kapoor," «The New York Times,» New York, 28 Sept. 1990;
- Justin Spring, "Anish Kapoor, Barbara Gladstone Gallery," «Artforum,» New York, Dec. 1990, p. 137;
- "New York in Review," «Arts Magazine,» Dec. 1990.

London, Tate Gallery, "Anish Kapoor. Drawings," 3 Oct.–10 Feb. 1991. Catalogue with text by Jeremy Lewison.
Works in exhibition: seventy-four untitled drawings, 1984–90, mixed media on paper.
- "Anish Kapoor's twin peaks," «Bazaar,» no. 15;
- John Russell Taylor, "Shapes and assemblies," «The Times,» London, 3 Oct. 1990;
- William Feaver, "Prize wake for timeless values," «The Observer,» London, 7 Oct. 1990;
- Marina Vaizey, "Seeing what comes naturally," «The Sunday Times,» London, 14 Oct. 1990;

- Sarah Kent, "Anish Kapoor," «Time Out,» London, 17 Oct. 1990;
- Stephanie du Tan, "Pigments of the imagination," «The Journal of Art,» Vol. 3, no. 2, London, Nov. 1990, pp. 31–33;
- Clair Frankel, "Watch where you walk at Tate," «International Herald Tribune,» 17 Nov. 1990;
- Bert Steevensz, "Anish Kapoor," «Metropolis M,» Feb. 1991, p. 48.

Grenoble, Le Magasin, Centre National d'Art Contemporain, 23 Nov.–19 Jan. 1991 (in collaboration with The British Council). Works in exhibition: *Tomb*, 1989, slate, pigment, 48.5x136x392 cm; *The Healing of St. Thomas*, 1989*; *It is Man*, 1989–90*; *Madonna*, 1989–90*; *Three Witches*, 1990, three elements, limestone, pigment, 192x113x89 cm, 202x125x88 cm, 204x110x90 cm; *Untitled (Seven Stones)*, 1990, limestone, dimensions variable; *Angel*, 1990, eleven elements, slate, pigment, dimensions variable; *Untitled*, 1990, Portland stone, 111x94x77 cm.
- Sylvie Perrard, "Quand la pierre devient immatérielle," «Dauphiné Libéré,» 22 Nov. 1990;
- Suzanne Engelson, "Du matériel à l'immatériel... A Grenoble," «Le Gutemberg,» 29 Nov. 1990;
- F.B., "Dark Heart," «The Art Newspaper,» no. 3, London, Dec. 1990;
- Philippe Gonnet, "L'essence de la matière," «Dauphiné Libéré,» 4 Dec. 1990;
- Nelly Gabriel, "Anish Kapoor, magicien et illusioniste," «Lyon Figaro,» Lyon, 4 Dec. 1990;
- Daniel Dobbels, "Kapoor: la forme de l'ineffable," «Libération,» 8 Dec. 1990;
- Geneviève Praplan, "Le désir et la croyance," «La Suisse,» 11 Dec. 1990;
- Bernadette Bost, "Le bleu de l'inconnu," «Le Monde Rhône-Alpes,» 15 Dec. 1990;
- Qg-T.T.D., "Les délices de Kapoor, non sans pigment," «Lyon Libération,» Lyon, 20 Dec. 1990;
- Jean Pagneux, "Les grands cimetières sous la lune," «L'Humanité,» 21 Dec. 1990;
- Claude Guilloteau, «Affiches de Grenobles et du Dauphiné,» 28 Dec. 1990;
- "L'art du silence," «La Suisse,» 31 Dec. 1990;
- J.J.No.,"Le trou noir du trou," «Grenoble Bimensuel,» Grenoble, 18 Dec. 1990–18 Jan. 1991;
- Philippe Piguet, "Monolithes et monochromes," «La Croix,» 15 Jan. 1991;
- "Anish Kapoor at Le Magasin," «Flash Art International,» Milan, Vol. XXIV, no. 156, Jan.–Feb. 1991, p. 147;
- Gloria Picazo, "Anish Kapoor," «Lapiz,» no. 75, Madrid, Feb. 1991.

1991

Madrid, Centro de Arte Reina Sofia, Palacio de Velázquez, 2 Feb.–17 April (in collaboration with The British Council). Catalogue (Spanish edition exhibition catalogue for XLIV Biennale di Venezia, 1990). Works in exhibition: *Void Field*, 1989*; *Tomb*, 1989*; *Madonna*, 1989–90*; *It is Man*, 1989–90*; *Three Witches*, 1990*; *Untitled*, 1990 [Le Magasin 1990, 111x94x77 cm]; *Angel*, 1990*; *Untitled (Seven Stones)*, 1990*; *The Earth*, 1991, mixed media, 102x102x91 cm.
- C.I. de Bustos, "Torres, Lupertz, Brossa y Kapoor: cita de la ultimas tendencias en el

CARS," «ABC Magazine,» 5 Feb. 1991, p. 50;
- "El Reina Sofia, en plena actividad," «El Punto,» 12 Feb. 1991, p. 18;
- "Torres, Lupertz, Kapoor y Brossa, en el Reina," «El Punto,» 14 Feb. 1991, p. 19;
- Juan Manuel Bonet, "Lupertz y Kapoor, dos voces europeas de los ochenta," «ABC Magazine,» 14 Feb. 1991, p. 126;
- F. Calvo Serraller, "Hacia el esplendor," «El Pais Magazine,» Madrid, 17 Feb. 1991, pp. 4–5;
- Maria Lluïsa Borràs,"Anish Kapoor exhibe esculturas de origine cromatismo en el palacio Velázquez," «La Vanguardia,» 18 Feb. 1991, p. 35;
- "Anish Kapoor, la escultura y el presente," «El Punto,» 8 March 1991;
- Pablo Llorca, "Literatura complicada, obra sencilla," «Diario 16,» 8 March 1991, p. 42.

Cologne, Feuerle Gallery, "Anish Kapoor & Ban Chiang," 15 Feb.–28 March. Catalogue with text by Angel Garcia.
Works in exhibition: *Void*, 1990, fibreglass, pigment, 92x92x78 cm; *Angel*, 1991, slate, pigment, 70x160x95 cm; *Void*, 1991, fibreglass, pigment, 93x129x95; five untitled drawings, 1987–90, mixed media on paper.
- Cornel Bierens, "Urformen der Kulturen," «Kolner Stadtanzeiger (KSTA),» Cologne, 21 March 1991;
- Beate Eickhoff, "Anish Kapoor und Gefäße der Ban–Chiang Kultur," «Kunstforum,» May–June 1991, pp. 365–366.

Hannover, Kunstverein, 10 May–14 June (in collaboration with The British Council). Catalogue.
Works in exhibition: *Tomb*, 1989*; *It Is Man*, 1989–90*; *Mountain*, 1989–90, fibreglass, earth, pigment, diam 208x182.8 cm; *Untitled*, 1990, three elements, fibreglass, pigment, diam 250x 167 cm each; *Three Witches*, 1990*; *Untitled*, 1991, sandstone, pigment, diam 152.4x156.2 cm.

Ushimado, "The Sixth Japan Ushimado International Art Festival".
Works in exhibition: *The Earth*, 1991*; *Untitled*, 1991, mixed media, dimensions variable.

1992

La Jolla, San Diego Museum of Contemporary Art, 1 Feb.–5 July 1992. Catalogue with texts by Lynda Forsha and Pier Luigi Tazzi. Works in exhibition: *The Healing of St. Thomas*, 1989*; *Untitled*, 1990, three elements, fibreglass, pigment, 250x170 cm ca. each; *Angel*, 1990, eight elements, slate, pigment, dimensions variable; *Untitled*, 1991, marble, 174x90x93 cm; *In the Presence of Form*, 1991, sandstone, 173x114x181 cm; *Pillar of Light*, 1991, sandstone, 152x153x143 cm; *The Earth*, 1991*; *When I am Pregnant*, 1992, mixed media, dimensions variable; *Untitled*, 1993, mixed media, pigment, dimensions variable, element: 19x14.3x1.3 cm.
Traveled to Des Moines, Des Moines Art Center, 30 Jan.–25 April 1993; Ottawa, The National Gallery of Canada, 18 June–19 Sept. 1993. Works in exhibition: *The Healing of St. Thomas*, 1989*; *Angel*, 1990*; *Three Witches*, 1990*; *Untitled*, 1990*; *In the Presence of Form*, 1991*; *Untitled*, 1991*; *Pillar of Light*, 1991*; *When I am Pregnant*, 1992*; The Power

Plant, Toronto, 19 Nov. 1993–2 Jan. 1994. Works in exhibition: *Pillar of Light*, 1989*; *The Healing of St. Thomas*, 1989*; *Angel*, 1990*; *Untitled*, 1990*; *In the Presence of Form*, 1991*; *Untitled*, 1991*; *When I am Pregnant*, 1992, mixed media, dimensions variable.
- Priscilla Lister, "Anish Kapoor: Contradictions say something," «San Diego Daily Transcript,» San Diego, 29 Jan. 1992;
- Susan Freudenheim, "Creating art from a diverse heritage," «San Diego County Los Angeles Times,» 30 Jan. 1992;
- Ann Jarmusch, "Dark and dangerous," «San Diego Tribune,» San Diego, 31 Jan. 1992;
- Robert L. Pincus, "Kapoor's fame far exceeds his ego," «The San Diego Union Tribune,» San Diego, 2 Feb. 1992;
- Kenneth Baker, "Between a rock and a soft place," «San Francisco Chronicle,» San Francisco, 26 Feb. 1992;
- Robert L. Pincus, "Sublime case of the blues," «San Diego Union-Tribune,» San Diego, 5 March 1992;
- Peter Clothier, "Metaphor or metaphysics, Jackie Winsor and Anish Kapoor," «Artspace,» Los Angeles, May–June 1992, pp. 44–49;
- Joseph Newland, "Spirit forms, Anish Kapoor at the Museum of Contemporary Art, San Diego," «Artweek,» 18 June 1992;
- Judith Christensen, "Anish Kapoor, San Diego Museum of Contemporary Art," «Sculpture,» July–Aug. 1992, p. 64;
- "San Diego, Kapoor at the MCA," «Flash Art International,» Milan, Vol. XXV, no. 166, Oct. 1992, p. 118;
- Jim Duncan, "Sculptor's granite caves pulls meditative viewers," «Des Moines Business Record,» Des Moines, 25 Jan. 1993;
- Eliot Nusbaum, "From floating stones to hollow tubes," «The Register,» Des Moines, Feb. 1993;
- Colette Tougas, "Anish Kapoor," «Parachute,» April–June 1993, pp. 30–31;
- Nancy Beale, "Two sculptors, two views of life," «The Ottawa Citizen,» Ottawa, 20 June 1993;
- Gillian MacKay, "British sculptor," «Canadian Art,» Summer 1993, p. 11;
- Nancy Beale, "Triple play at the National Gallery," «The Ottawa Citizen,» Ottawa, 20 June 1993;
- Nancy Beale, "Summer shows provide feast for all tastes," «The Ottawa Citizen,» Ottawa, 30 June 1993;
- Kate Taylor, "Healing visions carved in stone," «Globe and Mail,» Toronto, 5 July 1993;
- Ann Duncan, «The Gazette,» Ottawa, 16 July 1993;
- Lynda Forsha, "Anish Kapoor, Museum of Contemporary Art, San Diego," «Flash Art International,» Milan, Vol. XXVI, no. 168, Jan.–Feb. 1993, p. 132.

Madrid, Galeria Soledad Lorenzo, 28 April–30 May. Catalogue with text by José-Miguel Ullán. Works in exhibition: *Angel*, 1990, slate, pigment, 64x114x114 cm; *Untitled*, 1990–92, Forest of Dean sandstone, pigment, 195x107x88.9 cm; *Void*, 1991–1992, fibreglass, pigment, diam 165 cm ca.; *When I am Pregnant*, 1991–92, mixed media, diam 127x31.75 cm; *Untitled*, 1991–92, marble, 136.5x91.5x65.4 cm.
- Fietta Jarque, "La cultura monolítica europea ha dejado de existir, según el escultor

Le Magasin, Centre National d'Art Contemporain, Grenoble, 1990

Palacio Velázquez, Parque del Retiro, Centro de Arte Reina Sofia, Madrid, 1991

Palacio Velázquez, Parque del Retiro, Centro de Arte Reina Sofia, Madrid, 1991

Kunstverein Hannover, Hannover, 1991

Kunstverein Hannover, Hannover, 1991

223

Anish Kapoor," «El Pais,» Madrid/Barcelona, 27 April 1992;
- F. Calvo Serraller, "El arte del vacío," «El Pais,» Madrid/Barcelona, 27 April 1992;
- Betriz Pottecher, "Se ha puesto el gallo incierto, hombre," «El Mundo,» Madrid, 2 May 1992;
- Pablo Jiménez, "Anish Kapoor, entre el objeto y la pintura," «ABC de las artes,» Madrid, 8 May 1992;
- Fietta Jarque, "La experiencia de Anish Kapoor.'Cuando estoy embarazado'," «Guia de "El Pais",» Madrid, 8 May 1992;
- Jose Ramon Danvila, "Anish Kapoor, lo espiritual en la creación," «El Punto de las Artes,» Madrid, 8–14 May 1992, p. 5;
- Marcos R. Barnatán, "Un misterioso aerolito azul,"«El Mundo–Magazine,» Madrid, 9–10 May 1992;
- Ramón F. Reboiras and Miguel Fernandez, "La danza del cosmos," «Cambio 16,» Madrid, 10 May 1992, pp. 124–127;
- Rosa Olivares, "Anish Kapoor," «Lapiz,» no. 87, Madrid, May–June 1992, p. 74;
- Magdala Perpinyà, "Anish Kapoor, la irradiació del buit," «Papiers d'Art,» June–Aug. 1992, p. 19.

Los Angeles, Stuart Regen Gallery, Sept.–Oct.
Works in exhibition: *Untitled*, 1990* [Le Magasin 1990, 111x94x77 cm]; *Void*, 1992, fibreglass, pigment, 92x92x76.2 cm; *When I am Pregnant*, 1992*; *Untitled*, 1992, mixed media, dimensions variable.
- Susan Kandel, "The push and pull of Kapoor's metaphors," «Los Angeles Times,» Los Angeles, 9 Oct. 1992;
- Ralph Rugoff, "Depth of Field. Anish Kapoor's erotic pigments," «Los Angeles Weekly,» Los Angeles, 9–15 Oct. 1992.

1993
London, Lisson Gallery, 16 April–20 May.
Works in exhibition: *Icon*, 1992–93, mixed media, dimensions variable; *Passage*, 1993, sandstone, pigment, 169x172x134 cm; *Untitled*, 1993, mixed media, dimensions variable; *Untitled*, 1993, mixed media, dimensions variable; *In the Presence of Form II*, 1993, Portland stone, 175x201x122 cm; *Untitled*, 1993, mixed media, dimensions variable; *Eyes Turned Inward*, 1993, two elements, fibreglass, pigment, 155x155x135.5 cm each; *Bright Mountain*, 1993, fibreglass, paint, 140x231x147 cm; *Portrait of Light Picture of Space*, 1993, wood, paint, 198.5x107x5.2 cm; *Untitled*, 1993, plaster, pigment, 189.5x76.5x166 cm; three untitled drawings, 1993, mixed media on paper.
- Roger Bevan, "Kapoor at Lisson with stage designs," «The Art,» London, April 1993;
- Celia Lyttelton, "Anish Kapoor," «Interiors,» London, April 1993;
- Martin Gayford, "Watch this space," «Telegraph Magazine,» London, 10 April 1993, pp. 50–51;
- Richard Cork, "The shapeliness of things to come," «The Times,» London, 23 April 1993;
- Sarah Kent, "Shaping up," «Time Out,» London, 28 April 1993;
- Giles Auty, "Shock tactics," «Spectator,» London, 1 May 1993;
- William Feaver, "New life out of old wood," «The Observer,» London, 2 May 1993;
- John McEwen, "Anthony Green, Anish Kapoor, Alison Wilding, David Nash, and

Sutherland," «The Sunday Telegraph,» London, 2 May 1993;
- William Packer, "Never had it so good," «Financial Times,» London, 4 May 1993;
- Richard Dorment, "Body of work that cries out to be touched," «Daily Telegraph,» London, 5 May 1993;
- Simon Grant, "Anish Kapoor, Lisson Gallery," «What's On In London,» London, 12 May 1993;
- Leslee Wills, "Anish Kapoor, Lisson Gallery," «The Weekly Journal,» London, 13 May 1993;
- David Batchelor, "Anish Kapoor," «Galeries Magazine,» Paris, Summer 1993, p. 136;
- Marta Dalla Bernardina, "Lo spettatore e l'opera," «Segno,» no. 126, Summer 1993;
- Jeffrey Kastner, "Anish Kapoor, Lisson," «Flash Art International,» Milan, Vol. XXVI, no. 171, Summer 1993, p. 122;
- Keith Patrick, "Anish Kapoor, Lisson Gallery, London," «Art Line, International Art News,» Vol. 5, no. 8, Summer 1993;
- Claudia Peres, "Sculture da meditazione," «Casa Vogue,» Milan, July–Aug. 1993, pp. 54–57;
- "Anish Kapoor, Lisson," «Artnews,» New York, Oct. 1993, pp. 174–175.

Tel Aviv, Tel Aviv Museum of Art, 2 Sept.–6 Nov. Catalogue with text by Nehama Guralnik and a conversation between Anish Kapoor and Homi Bhabha.
Works in exhibition: *Tomb*, 1989*; *Angel*, 1990*; *When I am Pregnant*, 1992*; *Untitled*, 1992, sandstone, 188x107x67 cm; *Untitled: Void*, 1993, fibreglass, pigment, 155x155x135.5 cm; *Passage*, 1993*; *Untitled*, 1993* [Lisson 1993, 189.5x76.5x166 cm]; *Eyes Turned Inward*, 1993*.
- Felice Maranz, "Searching for the sacred Place," «The Jerusalem Report,» Jerusalem, 7 Oct. 1993.

New York, Barbara Gladstone Gallery, 27 Nov.–15 Jan. 1994.
Works in exhibition: *Bright Mountain*, 1993*; *Untitled*, 1993, fibreglass, pigment, diam 166.4x152.4 cm; *Untitled*, 1993, sandstone, 132x81x107 cm; *Untitled*, 1993, sandstone, 81x94x119 cm; *Untitled*, 1993, sandstone, 92x109x145 cm; *Untitled*, 1993, sandstone, 165x92x145 cm.
- "Exporama: Anish Kapoor," «Artpress,» no. 188, Feb. 1994, p. 72;
- Carol Kino, "Spiky peaks and shadowy voids," «Artnews,» New York, March 1994, p. 133;
- Donald Kuspit, "Anish Kapoor," «Artforum,» Vol. XXXII, no. 7 New York, March 1994, pp. 83–84.

1994
Ljubljana, Mala Galerija, Moderna Galerija Ljubljana, 13 May–12 June. Catalogue with text by Zdenka Badovinac.
Works in exhibition: *The Healing of St. Thomas*, 1989; *Untitled*, 1990–92, Forest of Dean sandstone, pigment, 195.5x107x88.9 cm; *Void*, 1991–92, fibreglass, pigment, diam 165.1x119.4 cm.

Nagoya, Kohji Ogura Gallery,"Echo," 21 Sept.–29 Oct. (in collaboration with Lisson Gallery, London).
Works in exhibition: *Echo*, 1993, five elements, wood, patinated bronze, ceramic, acrylic,

gouache, musical mechanism, 9x12.5x12.5 cm, 17x29.5x21 cm; diam 26x39.5, 10x28x24.5 cm, diam 14.5x24; thirteen untitled drawings, 1985–94, mixed media on paper.
- "Anish Kapoor," «Bijutsu Techo,» Japan, Jan. 1995, pp. 185–182.

1995
Tilburg, DePont Foundation, 11 March– 2 July. Catalogue.
Works in exhibition: *When I am Pregnant*, 1992*; *Untitled*, 1992, sandstone, pigment, 230x122x103 cm; *Untitled*, 1992, sandstone, pigment, 241x150x119 cm; *Untitled*, 1994–95, Kilkenny limestone, 202.5x140x125 cm; *Untitled*, 1994–95, limestone, 188x150x175 cm; *Untitled*, 1994–95, limestone, 180x136x100 cm; *Untitled*, 1994–95, wood, paint, 206x152.3x127.2 cm; *Untitled*, 1994–95, wood, paint, 206x152.6x127.8 cm; *Untitled*, 1995, aluminium, 149x98x99 cm; sixteen untitled drawings, 1994–95, mixed media on paper.
- Tony Godfrey, "Maastricht and Tilburg, the Bonnefanten Museum; Anish Kapoor," «The Burlington Magazine,» London, June 1995, pp. 407–408.

San Diego Museum of Contemporary Art, La Jolla, 1992

Lisson Gallery, London, 1993

Lisson Gallery, London, 1993

Tel Aviv Museum of Art, Tel Aviv, 1993

Group Exhibitions

1974
London, Serpentine Gallery, "Art into Landscape 1," 21 Sept.–20 Oct.

1975
London, Royal Academy of Art, "Young Contemporaries."

1978
Manchester, Whitworth Art Gallery, "Northern Young Contemporaries."

1979
Cambridge, Fitzwilliam Museum, "Tolly Cobbold: Eastern Arts, 2nd National Exhibition."

London, Whitechapel Art Gallery, "Whitechapel Open," Summer.

1980
Nottingham, Midland Group Gallery, "New Sculpture."

1981
London, Institute of Contemporary Art, "Objects & Sculpture: Richard Deacon, Antony Gormley, Anish Kapoor, Peter Randall-Page." Catalogue with texts by Lewis Biggs, Iwona Blazwick and Sandy Nairne. Traveled to Bristol, Arnolfini Gallery. [*Part of the Red*, 1981, five elements, earth, resin, pigment, dimensions variable].
- William Feaver, "An Air of Light Relief," «The Observer,» London, 26 June 1981.

London, Serpentine Gallery, "Summer Show," 12 Sept.–11 Oct.

London, Whitechapel Art Gallery, "British Sculpture in the 20th Century. Part 2: Symbol and Imagination 1951–80," 27 Nov.–24 Jan. 1982. Catalogue edited by Sandy Nairne and Nicholas Serota with texts by various authors. [*As if to Celebrate I Discovered a Mountain Blooming with Red Flowers*, 1981, five elements, wood, cement, polystyrene, pigment, 107x305x305 cm].

1982
Venice, Cantieri Navali della Giudecca, XL Biennale Internazionale di Venezia, "Aperto 82. Prima sezione-Tempo." Catalogue with text by Tommaso Trini.

Luzern, Kunstmuseum Luzern, "Englische Plastik Heute/British Sculpture Now," 11 July–12 Sept. Catalogue with texts by Martin Kunz, Michael Newman, *et al.*

Paris, Musée d'Art Moderne de la Ville de Paris and other seats, "XIIème Paris Biennale," 2 Oct.–14 Nov. Catalogue with texts by Georges Boudaille, Andrea Rose, *et al.*

Studio of the artist, London, 1979–80

Chambéry, Centre d'Art Contemporain, "Prefiguration."

London, Lisson Gallery, "London/New York 1982."

Oxford, Museum of Modern Art, "India: Myth and Reality."

Edinburgh, Fruitmarket Gallery, "Objects and Figures. New Sculpture in Britain," 20 Nov.–8 Jan. 1983 (organized by The Scottish Arts

Galerie Paul Maenz, Cologne, 1984

Council). Catalogue.

1983
Rennes, C'est Rien de le Dire, "Douceur de l'Avant-Garde," 7–29 Jan. Catalogue.

Gibellina, Museo Civico d'Arte Contemporanea, "Tema Celeste," 22 Jan.–30 March. Catalogue with text by Demetrio Paparoni.

Syracuse, Centro d'Arte Contemporanea, "La Trottola di Sirio," 29 Jan.–26 March (organized by The British Council). Catalogue with text by Demetrio Paparoni.

Southampton, John Hansard Gallery, "Figures and Objects," Feb.-March. Catalogue with text by Michael Newman.

Rotterdam, Rotterdamse Kunststichting, "Beelden/Sculpture 1983," 13 May-22 June. Catalogue with text by Paul Hefting.

Helsinki, "Finland Biennale."

Amsterdam, Van Krimpen Gallery, "Sculpture 1983," 28 May-25 June.

London, Hayward Gallery and Serpentine Gallery, "The Sculpture Show," 13 Aug.–9 Oct. (organized by The Arts Council of Great Britain). Catalogue with texts by Kate Blacker, Fenella Crichton, Paul de Monchaux, Nena Dimitrijevic, Stuart Morgan, Deanna Petherbridge, Bryan Robertson, Nicholas Wadley.
- Waldemar Januszczak, "Three into two won't go," «The Guardian,» London, 16 Aug. 1983;
- John Russell Taylor, "Playing into the hands of those who pour scorn," «The Times,» London, 16 Aug. 1983;
- Edward Lucie-Smith, "Back in touch with the emotions," «The Sunday Times,» London, 21 Aug. 1983;
- Mary Rose Beaumont, "The Sculpture Show," «Arts Review,» Sept. 1983.

London, Tate Gallery, "New Art," 14 Sept.–23 Oct. Catalogue.

Turin, Galleria Giorgio Persano, "Costellazione." Curated by Demetrio Paparoni.

Graz, Neue Galerie, "Eros Mythos Ironie," 17 Sept.–23 Oct. Catalogue with texts by Achille Bonito Oliva, Andrej Medved, Klaus Honnef, *et al.*

Sao Paulo, XVII Bienal de São Paulo, "Transformations: New Sculpture from Britain," 14 Oct.–18 Dec. (organized by The British Council). Catalogue with texts by Lewis Biggs, Lynne Cooke, Mark Francis, John McEwen, Stuart Morgan, Nicholas Serota, John Roberts. Traveled to Rio de Janeiro, Museu de Arte Moderna, 20 Jan.–20 Feb. 1984; Mexico City, Museo de Arte Moderna, 15 March–15 May 1984; Lisboa, Fundacão Calouste Gulbenkian, 1984.

1984
New York, Museum of Modern Art, "An International Survey of Recent Painting and Sculpture," 17 May–19 Aug. Catalogue with text by Kynaston McShine.
- John Russell, "Art: inaugural show is survey of new work," «The New York Times,» New York, 18 May 1984.

Cologne, Galerie Paul Maenz, "Anish Kapoor and Bill Woodrow," 6-30 June.

Dublin, the Guinness Hop Store, "ROSC '84." Catalogue.

Birmingham, Birmingham Museum and Art Gallery and Ikon Gallery, "The British Art Show: Old Allegiances and New Directions 1979–1984," 2 Nov.–22 Dec. (organized by The Arts Council of Great Britain). Catalogue with texts by Jon Thompson, Alexander Moffat and Marjorie Allthorpe-Guyton. Traveled to Edinburgh, Royal Scottish Academy, 19 Jan.–24 Feb.; Sheffield, Mappin Art Gallery, 16 March–4 May; Southampton Art Gallery, 18 May–30 June.

1985
"Sculptors' Drawings" (organized by The Scottish Arts Council). Traveled to Aberdeen, Artspace Galleries; Ayr, Lyth, Stirling, Stromness, Glasgow; Athen, Dracos Arts Centre.

Perth, Art Gallery of Western Australia, "The British Show" (organized by The Art Gallery of New South Wales and by The British Council), 19 Feb.–24 March. Catalogue with texts by John Roberts, Lewis Biggs, Graham Beal, Stuart Morgan, *et al.*
Traveled to Sydney, Art Gallery of New South Wales, 23 April–9 June; Brisbane, Queensland Art Gallery, 5 July–11 Aug.; Melbourne, The Exhibition Hall; Wellington, New Zeland, National Art Gallery.
- Ted Snell, "Relevance strikes a blow for the British," «The Australian,» Perth, 21 Feb. 1986.

Tubingen, Kunsthalle, "7000 Eichen," 2 March–14 April. Catalogue edited by Heiner Bastian. Traveled to Bielefeld, Kunsthalle, 2 June–11 Aug.

Boston, Institute of Contemporary Art, "Currents," 3 April. Catalogue with text by David Joselit.

Paris, "Nouvelle Biennale de Paris." Catalogue with texts by Georges Boudaille, Stuart Morgan, *et al.*

Bologna, Galleria Comunale d'Arte Moderna and other seats, "Anniottanta," 4 July–30 Sept. Catalogue with texts by Renato Barilli, Flavio Caroli, Concetto Pozzati, Claudio Spadoni, Lynne Cooke, *et al.*

Bristol, Arnolfini Gallery, "Who's Afraid of Red, Yellow and Blue?," 31 Aug.–6 Oct.

State University of New York, Neuberger Museum, "Three British Sculptors."

Tournus, l'Abbaye de Tournus, "20 Sculptures du FRAC Rhône-Alpes."

Chicago, Donald Young Gallery, "Anish Kapoor and Bill Woodrow." [*Mother as a Mountain*, 1985, wood, chalk, pigment, 145x200x145 cm].

Dublin, Douglas Hyde Gallery, "The Poetic Object: Richard Deacon, Shirazeh Houshiary, Anish Kapoor," 21 Nov.–21 Dec. Catalogue with text by Richard Francis. Traveled to Belfast, The Arts Council Gallery, 9 Jan.–1 Feb. 1986.
- Aidan Dunne, "Ambiguous objects just being themselves," «The Sunday Press,» 24 Nov. 1985;
- Bruce Arnold, "Close look at new British sculpture," «The Independent on Sunday,» London, 24 Nov. 1985;
- Brian Fallon, "'The Poetic Object' at TCD," «The Irish Times,» Dublin, 28 Nov. 1985.

1986
Madrid, Palacio de Velázquez, "Entre el objeto y la imagen. Escultura Britanica contemporanea," 28 Jan.–30 April (organized by The British Council and Ministerio Español de Cultura). Catalogue with texts by Lewis Biggs and Juan Muñoz. Traveled to Barcelona, Centre Cultural de la Caixa de Pensions, "Entre l'objecte i la imatge," 3 June–17 July 1986. Catalogue.

Humlebaek, Louisiana Museum of Modern Art, "Skulptur-9 Kunstnere fra Storbrittanien," 1 March–20 April. Catalogue.

Arnhem, Holland, Park Sonsbeek, "Sonsbeek '86. International Sculpture Exhibition," 18 June–14 Sept. Catalogue in two volumes with texts by G. F. Boreel, Saskia Bos, Antje von Graevenitz, Marianne Brouwer and statements by the artists.
[*Pot for Her*, 1985, pigment, mixed media, 269x104x104 cm; *Untitled*, 1986, three elements, wood, chalk, h max 300 cm].

Buffalo, Albright-Knox Art Gallery, "General Idea, Anish Kapoor, Melissa Miller," 12 July–24 Aug. Catalogue with text by Helen Raye.

Frankfurt, Frankfurter Kunstverein and Schirn Kunsthalle Frankfurt, "Prospect '86. Eine internationale Austellung aktueller Kunst," 9 Sept.–2 Nov. Catalogue.

New York, Lang & O'Hara Gallery, "Inaugural Exhibition."

Paris, Galerie Gabrielle Maubrie, "Dessins de Sculpteurs," 24 Sept.–24 Oct.

1987
Stockholm, Liljevalchs Konstall, "British Art of the 1980s," 10 April–24 May (organized by The British Council). Catalogue with text by Lynne Cooke. Traveled to Tampere, Sara Hildén Art Museum, "Britannia. Paintings and Sculptures from the 1980s," 16 June–23 Aug. 1987.

Long Island, P.S. 1, The Institute for Art and Urban Resources, "Juxtapositions: Recent Sculpture from England and Germany," 26 April–21 June. Catalogue with texts by Alanna Heiss, Joshua Decter, Denys Zacharopoulos.

London, Serpentine Gallery, "Vessel," 5 Sept.–11 Oct.
[*Here and There*, 1987, Cotswold sandstone, pigment, 90x246.5x160 cm].

Antwerpen, Museum Van Hedendaagse Kunst,

Studio of the artist, London, 1985

Rijksmuseum Kröller-Müller, Otterlo, 1990

"Inside/Outside," Catalogue.

Dusseldorf, Kunsthalle, "Similia-Dissimilia," curated by Rainer Crone. Catalogue with text by Cornelia Lauf. Traveled to New York, Columbia University, 4 Dec.–30 Jan. 1988, Sonnabend Gallery and Leo Castelli Gallery, 5–22 Dec.

Brussels, Musée d'Art Moderne, "Viewpoint. L'art contemporain en Grande Bretagne," 18 Dec.–31 Jan. 1988 (in collaboration with The British Council). Catalogue with an interview by Richard Cork.

1988
Prato, Museo d'Arte Contemporanea Luigi Pecci, "Europa oggi/Europe now," 25 June–20 Oct. Catalogue with texts by Amnon Barzel, Achille Bonito Oliva, Bruno Corà, Helmut Draxler, Antje van Gravenitz, Joseph Kosuth, Donald Kuspit, Jean-Hubert Martin, Beatrice Merz, Carlo Bertelli, Gillo Dorfles, Knud Jensen, Peter Ludwig, Thomas M. Messer, Giuseppe Panza di Biumo, *et al.*

Nuremberg, Kunsthalle, "Fourth International Drawing Triennale," 1–23 Oct. Catalogue with text by David Reason.

Lyon, Musée St. Pierre, "La Couleur seule. L'Experience du Monochrome," 7 Oct.–5 Dec. Catalogue with texts by Thierry Raspail, Maurice Besset, Thomas McEvilley, Thierry de Duve, *et al.*
[*Mother as a Void*, 1988, fibreglass, pigment, 205x205x230 cm].

Le Havre, Musée des Beaux-Arts André Malraux; Rouen, École d'Architecture de Normandie; Évreux, Musée de l'Éveche, "Britannica," 15 Oct.–12 Dec. Catalogue with texts by Catherine Grenier, Francoise Cohen and Lynne Cooke. Traveled to Antwerpen, Museum Van Hedendaagse, Jan.–March 1989; Labege Innopole, Centre Regional d'Art Contemporain, March–May 1989.
- F. Bataillon, "Britannica," *Artpress*, no. 131, Dec. 1988, p. 64.

Liverpool, Tate Gallery, "Starlit Waters. British Sculpture: An International Art 1968–88." Catalogue with text by Martin Kunz, Charles Harrison and Lynne Cooke.

Pittsburgh, The Carnegie Museum of Art, "Carnegie International." Catalogue with text by Kellie Jones.
[*Blood Stone*, 1988, two elements, limestone, pigment, 211x83.3x61 cm, 83.8x89x109.2 cm].

Montreal, Musée d'art contemporain de Montréal, "British Now: sculpture et autres dessins." Catalogue with text by Sandra Grant Marchand.

1989
Paris, Galerie Le Gall Peyroulet, "Anish Kapoor, Wolfgang Laib, Richard Long," 6 June–22 July.

1990
Chicago, The Art Institute of Chicago, "Affinities and Intuitions. The Gerald S. Elliott Collection of Contemporary Art," 12 May–29 July. Catalogue curated by Neal Benezra, with texts by Lynne Cooke, Mark Rosenthal, *et al.*

Tokyo, Setagaya Museum, "British Art Now: A Subjective View," 25 Aug.–7 Oct. (organized by The British Council). Catalogue with texts by H. M. Hughes, J. Shioda, A. Graham-Dixon, A. Obigane. Traveled to Fukuoka, Fukuoka Art Museum, 1990; Nagoya, Nagoya City Art Museum, 1990; Tochigi, Tochigi Prefectural Museum of Fine Arts, 1991; Hyogo, Hyogo Prefectural Museum of Modern Art, 1991; Hiroshima, Hiroshima City Museum of Contemporary Art, 1991.

Otterlo, Holland, Rijksmuseum Kröller-Müller, "Dujourie, Fortuyn, Houshiary, Kapoor," 14 Sept.–29 Oct. Catalogue with text by Marianne Brouwer.
[*Untitled*, 1990, triptych, fibreglass, pigment, diam 250x167 cm each].

Gstaad, Switzerland, Galerie Saqqarah, "Heroes of Contemporary Art," 17 Nov.–15 Jan. 1991. Catalogue with text by Akim Monet. Traveled to Cologne, TransArt Exhibitions Kreishaus.

London, Frith Street Gallery, "Works on paper," 23 Nov.–22 Dec.

Brussels, Galerie Isy Brachot, "Made of Stone," 19 Dec.–26 Jan. 1991. Catalogue.

1991
Kyoto, Gallery Shirakawa.

Fréjus, Fondation Daniel Templon, "La sculpture contemporaine après 1970," 4 July–29 Sept. Catalogue with texts by C. Ratcliff, P. Cabanne, D. Dobbels, S. Gohr, D. Paparoni, C. Smulders.

Malmö, Rooseum, "Trans/Mission," 27 Aug.–27 Oct. Curated by Lars Nittve. Catalogue with texts by Lars Nittve and Dick Hebdige.

London, Tate Gallery, "The 1991 Turner Prize: An Exhibition of Work by the Four Shortlisted Artists," 6 Nov.–8 Dec. Catalogue with text by Sean Rainbird.
- Iain Gale and Dalya Alberge, "Youth and beauty?," «The Independent,» London, 16 July 1991;
- Richard Dorment, "A prize turnabout," «Daily Telegraph,» London, 16 July 1991;
- Tom Lubbock, "Shortlist short on ideas," «The Independent on Sunday,» London, 21 July 1991;
- Stuart Morgan, "The Turner Prize," «Frieze,» London, Oct., pp. 4–8;
- Richard Dorment, "A winner in a class of his own," «Daily Telegraph,» London, 27 Nov. 1991;
- Roger Bevan, "Controversy over the Turner Prize short-list," «The Art Newspaper,» no. 12, London, Nov. 1991, p. 3;
- Sarah Kent, "Prize Fighters," «Time Out,» London, Nov. 1991;
- "Turner Prize for Anish Kapoor," «Indian Weekly,» Dec. 1991;
- Roger Bevan, "Anish Kapoor wins Turner Prize," «The Art Newspaper,» London, 14 Jan. 1992.

The Hague, Haags Gemeentemuseum, "Rhizome," 26 Nov.–19 Jan. 1992. Catalogue.
- Els van der Plas, "Rhizome, a rootstock that offers no hold, Haags Gemeentemuseum," «Kunst and Museum Journal,» no. 4, pp. 60–62.

Milan, Studio Oggetto, "Il limite delle cose nella Nuova Scultura Inglese," Nov.–Dec. Catalogue with texts by Enrico Pedrini and Emilio Stabilini.

Fukuoka, Fukuoka Art Museum, "Anish Kapoor and Abstract Art in Asia."

1992
New York and San Francisco, Crown Point Press, "Prints by Sculptors. Anish Kapoor and Jane Provisor."
- B.A.M., "Anish Kapoor, Jannis Provisor-Crown Point Press," «Artnews,» New York, April, pp. 119–120;
- David Bonetti, "Risk-taking artists find their Crowning Point," «The San Francisco Examiner,» 27 May 1992.

Kassel, "Documenta IX," 13 June–20 Sept. Catalogue in three volumes with texts by Wolfram Bremeier, Jan Hoet, Denys Zacharopoulos, Bart De Baere, Pier Luigi Tazzi, Claudia Herstatt, Joyce Carol Oates, Jacques Roubaud, Cornelius Castoriadis, Heiner Muller, Paul Robbrecht, Hilde Daem.
[*Descent into Limbo*, 1992, concrete, stucco, 600x600x600 cm].
- "Documenta IX images," «Artefactum,» Antwerpen, Sept.–Nov. 1992;
- Grazia Toderi, "The light of the sun will reveal it," «Flash Art International,» vol. XXV, no. 166, Milan, Oct. 1992, p. 134.

University of North Texas Art Gallery, "The New British Sculpture. Selected works from the Patsy R. and Raymond D. Nasher Collection." Catalogue.

London, Whitechapel Art Gallery, "Whitechapel Open," 19 June–28 Aug.

Tilburg, De Pont Foundation for Contemporary Art, "De Opening," 13 Sept.–31 Jan. 1993. Catalogue.
[*Untitled*, 1992, fibreglass, acrylic, pigment, diam 100 cm; *Untitled*, 1992, polystyrene, aluminium, fibreglass, acrylic, pigment, diam 220 cm].

Brussels, Centre de Conférences Albert Borschette, "New Voices, New Works for the British Council Collection," 23 Sept.–Dec. (organized by The British Council). Catalogue with text by Gill Hedley.

Verona, Foro per l'Arte Contemporanea, "Anish Kapoor invita Gary Woodley," 17 Oct.–29 Nov. Catalogue with texts by Erno Vroonen and Paolo Gambazzi.
- Jos van den Bergh, "Anish Kapoor, Gary Woodley," «Artefactum,» Antwerpen, Dec. 1992–Jan. 1993, pp. 55–56.

Amsterdam, Stedelijk Museum.

Mito-shi Ibaraki, Japan, Art Tower Mito, "Another World," 21 Nov.–7 March 1993. Catalogue with text by Yoko Hasegawa.
[*Dragon*, 1992, eleven elements, limestone, pigment, dimensions variable].

1993
Derby, Derby Museum and Art Gallery, "British Sculpture from the Arts Council Collection" (organized by The Arts Council of Great Britain). Catalogue with text by James Roberts.
- Clare Henry, "Terrific sculptures but none by Scots," «Glasgow Herald,» Glasgow, 28 May 1993;
- Andrew Gibbon Williams, "Parts for art's sake," «The Sunday Times (Scottish Section),» 30 May 1993.

Venice, Giardini di Castello, Padiglione Italia, XLV Esposizione Internazionale d'Arte, "Punti dell'arte. Aureo," 14 June–10 Oct. Catalogue (vol. 1) with texts by Arthur C. Danto and Tommaso Trini.
[*My Body Your Body*, 1993, fibreglass, pigment, dimensions variable, element: 248x103x205 cm].
- Alison Sarah Jacques, "Anish Kapoor, the distance between 'here' and 'there'," «Flash Art Daily,» Venice, June 1993;
- Thomas McEvilley, "Venice the Menace," «Artforum,» Vol. XXXII, no. 2, New York, Oct. 1993.
Venice, Collezione Peggy Guggenheim, XLV Esposizione Internazionale d'Arte, "Art Against Aids." Catalogue (vol. 2) with text by John Cheim, Diego Cortez, Carmen Gimenez, Klaus Kertess.
Venice, Isola di San Lazzaro degli Armeni, Monastero Mechitarista. "Trésors de voyage" (supported by La Biennale di Venezia). Catalogue (vol. 2) with text by Adelina von Furstenberg.

New York, Leo Castelli Gallery, "Sculpture."

Sheffield, Graves Art Gallery, "Body of Drawings" (organized by The South Bank Centre). Traveled to Coventry, Mead Art Gallery.

Óbidos, Portogallo, Bienal Internacional de Óbidos, "Cerco," 9 Oct.–27 Nov. Catalogue.
[*Black Stones, Human Bones*, 1993, two elements, marble, 131x163x171.5 cm, diam 90 cm].

Vienna, Architectur Zentrum, "Magazin," 22 Nov.–13 Dec.

1994
Cologne, Hohenthal und Bergen, "Punishment and Decoration," 8 April–28 May. Catalogue with text by Michael Corris.

London, Tate Gallery, "Sculptors' Drawings," 5 July–30 Oct.

Hiroshima, Hiroshima City Museum of Contemporary Art, "Asian Art Now," 18 Sept.–6 Nov.

S. Antonino di Susa (Turin), Stabilimento Radiomarelli, "Collezione Re Rebaudengo-Sandretto," 24 Sept.–18 Nov.

St. Petersburg, Russian Museum, "A Changing World: Fifty Years of Sculpture from the British Council Collection," 17 Oct.–28 Nov. Catalogue. Traveled to Moscow, New Tretyakov, 28 April–26 May 1995; Prague, Castle Riding Hall, 27 June–1 Oct. 1995.

1995
Helsinki, Museum of Contemporary Art, "Ars '95 Helsinki," 11 Feb.–28 May.

Edinburgh, Scottish National Gallery of Modern Art, "Contemporary British Art in Print," 25 Feb.–30 April. Catalogue. Traveled to New Haven, Yale Center for British Art, 2 Dec.–4 Feb. 1996.

Dublin, The Irish Museum of Modern Art, "British Art of the 1980s & 1990s. Works from The Weltkunst Collection," 18 May–5 Oct.
- Brian Fallon, "British sculpture here and now," «The Irish Times,» Dublin, 18 May 1995.

Modena, Galleria Civica, Palazzo dei Giardini, "Arte inglese d'oggi nella raccolta Re-Rebaudengo Sandretto," 21 May–30 July. Curated by Flaminio Gualdoni and Gail Cochrane. Catalogue with text by Flaminio Gualdoni.

Santiago de Compostela, Auditorio de Galicia, "De Henry Moore ós anos 90. Escultura británica contemporánea," 3 June–25 July. Catalogue. Traveled to Oporto, Fundacão Serralves, 7 Sept.–5 Nov.

Santa Fe, Museum of Fine Arts and SITE, "Longing and Belonging: From the Faraway Nearby," 14 July–8 Oct.
- Charles Dee Mitchell, "Introducing SITE Santa Fe," «Art in America,» 83, no. 10, pp. 44–47.

London, Lisson Gallery, "Ideal Standard Summertime," 17 July–30 Sept.

- Sarah Kent, "Summer Frieze," «Time Out,» no. 1301, London, 26 July–2 Aug. 1995, p. 50;
- Rosanna Negrotti, "Ideal Standard Summertime," «What's On In London,» London, 9 Aug. 1995, p. 21;
- Richard Cork, "Summer brings cold comfort," «The Times,» London, 15 Aug. 1995;
- Linda Talbot, "Threads of many ideas," «Hampstead & Highgate Express,» London, 18 Aug. 1995.

London, Flowers East, "British Abstract Art Part II: Sculpture," 5 Aug.–3 Sept. 1995.
- Martin Gayford, "The subject is anything," «The Daily Telegraph,» London, 16 Aug. 1995.

Collaborations

1992

Seville, Expo'92. "Building for A Void."
Architectural collaboration with David Connor.
- "Anish Kapoor/David Connor," «SD. Art
and Public Space.»
- "Journey to the centre of a void,"
«The Independent,» London, 8 January 1992.
- David Cohen, "Anish Kapoor," «Sculpture,»
Washington, January–February 1992,
pp. 30–37.
- Roger Bevan, "American art-less in Seville:
Britain fields four sculptors," «The Art
Newspaper», no. 17, London, April 1992.
- Giles Tremlett, "Seville's Expo '92," «The
Times,» London, 12 August 1992.

1993

London, Queen Elizabeth Hall. "River Run."
Stage design for dance performance.
A collaboration with Laurie Booth and Hans
Peter Kuhn.
- Judith Mackrell, "Rock and Roll. The rising
fall of Laurie Booth," «Vogue,» London,
February 1993.
- Jacqui Bealing, "Putting a spring into
dancer's steps," «Brighton Evening Argus,»
East Sussex, 15 March 1993.
- Sophie Constanti, "Laurie Booth, Queen
Elizabeth Hall," «The Guardian,» London,
29 March 1993.
- Judith Mackrell, "Laurie Booth's *River Run*,
with designs by Anish Kapoor, at Queen
Elizabeth Hall," «The Independent,» London,
31 March 1993.
- "Main Chance," «Sheffield Telegraph,»
Sheffield, 14 May 1993.
- Nicholas Dromgoole, "Preferable to
prison?," «The Sunday Telegraph,» London,
4 April 1993.
- Jann Parry, "Dance," «The Observer,»
London, 4 April 1993.
- Anne Sacks, "Calm in an arctic limbo,"
«The Independent on Sunday,» London,
4 April 1993.
- Jane King, "Meaningless meanderings,"
«The Morning Star,» London, 18 April 1993.
- "Dance, sound and sculpture," «Somerset
County Gazette,» Taunton, 23 April 1993.
- Cathy Brown, "Rare treat in store for dance
fans at famous concert hall," «What's On In
London,» London, May 1993.

1994

Echo. A group of five sculptures which
incorporate music mechanisms.
A collaboration with the composer Brian Elias.

Selected Bibliography

For each section, chronological arrangement

Writings, Statements, and Projects for Periodicals and Catalogues by the Artist
- "The works are about sensuality...," in *Sonsbeek 86*, exhibition catalogue, Utrecht, Veen/Reflex, 1986, p. 328;
- Anish Kapoor, Sylvie Primard, Pier Luigi Tazzi. "Mother as a Mountain," project for «Artforum,» New York, September 1989, pp. 126–131.

Interviews
Demetrio Paparoni. "Spazio di Dio, spazio della Terra," «Tema Celeste,» no. 6, Syracuse, 1985, pp. 46–49;

Richard Cork. In "Anish Kapoor: Works on Paper 1975–1987," exhibition catalogue, Sidney, Ray Hughes Gallery, 1987;

Mileta Prodanovic. "Anish Kapoor, Razgovor," «Moment,» no. 15, July-September 1989, pp. 16–18;

Ameena Meer. "Anish Kapoor," «BOMB,» no. 30, Winter, 1989–90, pp. 38–43;

Akio Obigane. "Anish Kapoor," «Atelier,» no. 755, January 1990, pp. 2–24;

Paul Taylor. "Anish Kapoor," «Interview,» New York, June 1990, p. 93;

"Anish Kapoor interviewed by Douglas Maxwell," «Art Monthly,» London, May 1990, pp. 6–12;

Doris Van Drateln. "Anish Kapoor, Ein Gespräch," «Kunstforum,» vol. 109, August–October 1990, pp. 304–315;

Caroline Smulders. "Anish Kapoor. Vers la dématérialisation de l'objet," «Artpress,» no. 152, November 1990, pp. 16-21;

Stephanie du Tan. "Pigments of the Imagination," «The Journal of Art,» vol. 3, no. 2, London, November 1990, pp. 31–33;

Yoshiko Ikoma. "Anish Kapoor: Interview," «Crea,» no. 5, 1991;

Constance Lewallen. "Interview with Anish Kapoor, Japan, September, 1990," «View,» vol. VII, no. 4, San Francisco, Fall 1991, pp. 2–32;

Pablo Llorca. "Anish Kapoor, 'Mi madre are judía; mi padre, hindú; mi nana, cristiana; mi profesor, budista'," «Diario 16,» Madrid, 10 May 1992;
Alison Sarah Jacques. "Anish Kapoor, the distance between 'here' and 'there'," «Flash Art Daily,» Venice, June 1993;

Francesco Bonami. "Jumping into the Void," «Flash Art International,» vol. XXVII, no. 179, Milan, November–December 1994, pp. 81–82.

Books, Solo Exhibition Catalogues
Anish Kapoor. Beeldhouwwerken, Rotterdam, Galerie 't Venster, 1983. Text by Michael Newman;

Feeling into Form, Liverpool, Walker Art Gallery and Lyon, Le Nouveau Musée, 1983. Text by Marco Livingstone;

Anish Kapoor, Basel, Kunsthalle, 1985. Texts by Jean-Christophe Ammann, Alexander von Grevenstein, Ananda Coomaraswamy;

Anish Kapoor, Oslo, Kunstnernes Hus, 1986. Texts by Arne Malmedal, Lynne Cooke;

Anish Kapoor: Recent Sculpture and Drawings, Amherst, University Gallery, Fine Arts Center, University of Massachusetts, 1986. Text by Helaine Posner;

Anish Kapoor: Works on Paper 1975–1987, Sydney, Ray Hughes Gallery, 1987;

Anish Kapoor, Nagoya, Japan, Kohji Ogura Gallery and London, Lisson Gallery, 1989. Text by Pier Luigi Tazzi;

Anish Kapoor. British Pavilion, XLIV Venice Biennale, London, The British Council, 1990. Texts by Thomas McEvilley, Marjorie Allthorpe-Guyton;

Marco Livingstone, ed. *Anish Kapoor*, Kyoto, Art Random, Kyoto Shoin International, 1990;

Anish Kapoor. Drawings, London, Tate Gallery, 1990. Text by Jeremy Lewison;

Anish Kapoor, Madrid, Centro de Arte Reina Sofia and The British Council (Spanish edition exhibition catalogue XLIV Biennale di Venezia), 1991;

Anish Kapoor, Hannover, Kunstverein and The British Council, 1991;

Anish Kapoor & Ban Chiang, Cologne, Feuerle, 1991. Text by Angel Garcia;

Anish Kapoor, San Diego Museum of Contemporary Art, 1992. Texts by Lynda Forsha, Pier Luigi Tazzi;

Anish Kapoor, Madrid, Galeria Soledad Lorenzo, 1992. Text by José-Miguel Ullán;

Anish Kapoor, Tel Aviv, Tel Aviv Museum of Art, 1993. Introduction by Nehama Guralnik and a conversation between Anish Kapoor and Homi Bhabha;

Anish Kapoor, Ljubljana, Moderna Galerija, 1994. Text by Zdenka Badovinac.

Articles and Essays About the Artist
Michael Newman. "Le drame du désir dans la sculpture d'Anish Kapoor," «Artpress,» no. 70, May 1983, pp. 31–33;

Patrick Kinmouth. "Anish Kapoor's Shades of Meaning," «Vogue,» August 1983, pp. 104–107;

Michelangelo Castello. "Se il vero prende corpo," «Tema Celeste,» vol. 1, Syracuse, November 1983, pp. 12–15;

Robin Dutt. "Anish Kapoor," «New Life,» no. 346, 18 November 1983;

"Sculptor Anish Kapoor," «Art Gallery,» December 1984–January 1985, p. 33;

Lynne Cooke. "Mnemic Migrations," «Louisiana Revy,» no. 2, March 1986, pp. 28–32;

"Anish Kapoor," «Lapiz,» Madrid, no. 42, 1987, p. 57;

Kosme Maria de Barañano. "Anish Kapoor-Towards the Point of Origin," «Lapiz,» no. 78, Madrid, June 1991, pp. 28–35;

Liliane Touraine. "Anish Kapoor. De la modification pour principe à un symbolisme de l'universal," «Artefactum,» vol. 8, no. 38, April-May 1991, pp. 9–11;

Farida Cooper. "Anish Kapoor," «Society,» Bombay, January 1992, pp. 50–55;

Marta Dalla Bernardina. "Erotismo e trascendenza nella scultura di Anish Kapoor," «Palazzo Ruini,» Reggio Emilia, October–November–December 1992, pp. 4–5;

David Cohen. "Anish Kapoor," «Sculpture,» Washington, January-February, pp. 30–37;

Geraldine Norman. "Sculptor creates fibreglass vision," «The Independent,» London, 10 May 1993;

"Anish Kapoor," «Art Watching (Freestyle),» vol. 45, no. 666, Winter 1993;

John K. Grande. "Anish Kapoor," «Espace,» no. 25, Montreal, Fall 1994, pp. 27–32.

General Reference Books, Catalogues and Articles
Andrea Rose. "Odd Couples," «London Magazine,» London, September 1982, pp. 107–113;

Michael Newman. "New Sculpture in Britain," «Art in America,» September 1982, pp. 104–114, 177, 179;

Michael Newman. "Figuren und Objekte. Neue Skulptur in England," «Kunstforum,» no. 62, June 1983, pp. 22–35;

Hayward Annual, exhibition catalogue (with a conversation between Stuart Morgan and Kate Blacker), London, Hayward Gallery, South Bank Centre, 1983;

Michael Newman. "Discourse and Desire: Recent British Sculpture," «Flash Art International,» no. 115, Milan, January 1984, pp. 48–55;

Elisabeth Vedrenne. "L'illusion du désir," «Décoration Internationale,» Paris, no. 85, October 1985, pp. 41–44;

Paul Bonaventura. "An Introduction to Recent British Sculpture," «Artefactum,» September–October 1987;

Richard Cork. «Kunstschrift,» 1987, p. 224;

Terry A. Neff, ed. *A Quiet Revolution: British Sculpture Since 1965*, London, Thames & Hudson, 1987;

Edward Lucie-Smith. *Sculpture since 1945*, London, Phaidon Press, 1987;

Sarah Jane Checkland. "No critics please, they're British," «The Times,» London, 2 October 1990;

William Feaver. "View down the grant-aid road," «The Observer,» London, 30 December 1990;

Jan Donia, ed. *Surrogaat/Surrogate. 15 years of Galerie 't Venster from Kiefer to Koons.* Texts by Jan Donia, Wofgang Max Faust, Rotterdam, SDU Uitgeverij, 1990;

Hans Gercke, ed. *Blau: Farbe der Ferne,* exhibition catalogue, Heidelberg, Wunderhorn, 1990;

Kenneth Baker. "Sculptors Go Two-Dimensional,"«The San Francisco Chronicle,» San Francisco, 20 February 1991;

Paul Overy. "Lions and Unicorns: The Britishness of Postwar British Sculpture," «Art in America,» September 1991;

Henry Meyric Hughes. "Art Exports," «Art Review Yearbook,» London, 1991, pp. 32–34;

Francesca Borelli. "Sculture che sigillano il secolo," «Wimbledon,» Rome, February 1992, pp. 71–74;

Roger Bevan. "New contemporary art fair opens in Japan," «The Art Newspaper,» London, March 1992;

Geraldine Norman. "Eighties for sale," «The Independent on Sunday,» London, 3 May 1992;

Raghubir Singh. "Banaras Transformed," «Sunday,» Calcutta/London, 1-7 November 1992, pp. 86–89;

Kate Bernard. "Which way to Turner?," «The Sunday Times,» London, 25 July 1993;

Jeremy Isaacs. "A sense of the future," «Modern Painters,» London, July 1993;

Martin Gayford. "Forms that rhyme," «Sunday Telegraph,» London, 5 September 1993;

Colin Glaedell. "Still Tough at the Top," «Art Monthly,» London, June 1994, pp. 177–178;

Fiona Giannulis. "Soul Mates," «The Telegraph Magazine,» London, 23 July 1994;

"Artistas Extranjeros Adquisiciones, Donaciones y Daciones," «La Revista del Museo, Museo Nacional Centro de Arte Reina Sofia,» Madrid, July 1994, pp. 20–23;

Simon Corbin. "Sculptors' Drawings," «What's On in London,» London, 24 August 1994, p. 19;

F.F. "Per la regina e per i Re," «Il Giornale dell'Arte,» no. 126, October 1994;

"Luis Monreal, Director of La Caixa, Has a National Sized Budget to Spend," «The Art Newspaper,» International Edition, Londra, vol. V, no. 41, October 1994;

Adrian Searle. "We Know You are in There," «The Independent,» London, 4 November 1994;

"Die 100 Grobten," «Capital,» no. 11, Cologne, November 1994, pp. 173–174;

Pilar Corrias. "Looking to the future: contemporary art in London," «The Society of Londra Art Dealers (1994/95 Yearbook & Directory of Members),» London, 1994, pp. 44–45;

"Old Masters and Young Pretenders," «Time Out Visitors Guide 1994,» London, 1994, pp. 33–36;

Nicolas De Oliveira, Michael Petry, Nicola Oxley, eds. *Installation Art*, London, Thames & Hudson, 1994;

Patricia Bickers. "La sculpture britannique: générations et tradition," «Art press,» no. 202, May 1995, pp. 31–39;

Jonathan Fineberg. *Art since 1940. Strategies of Being,* Englewood Cliffs, Prentice Hall, 1995.